AF413426

TECLA TOFANO
THIS BODY OF MINE

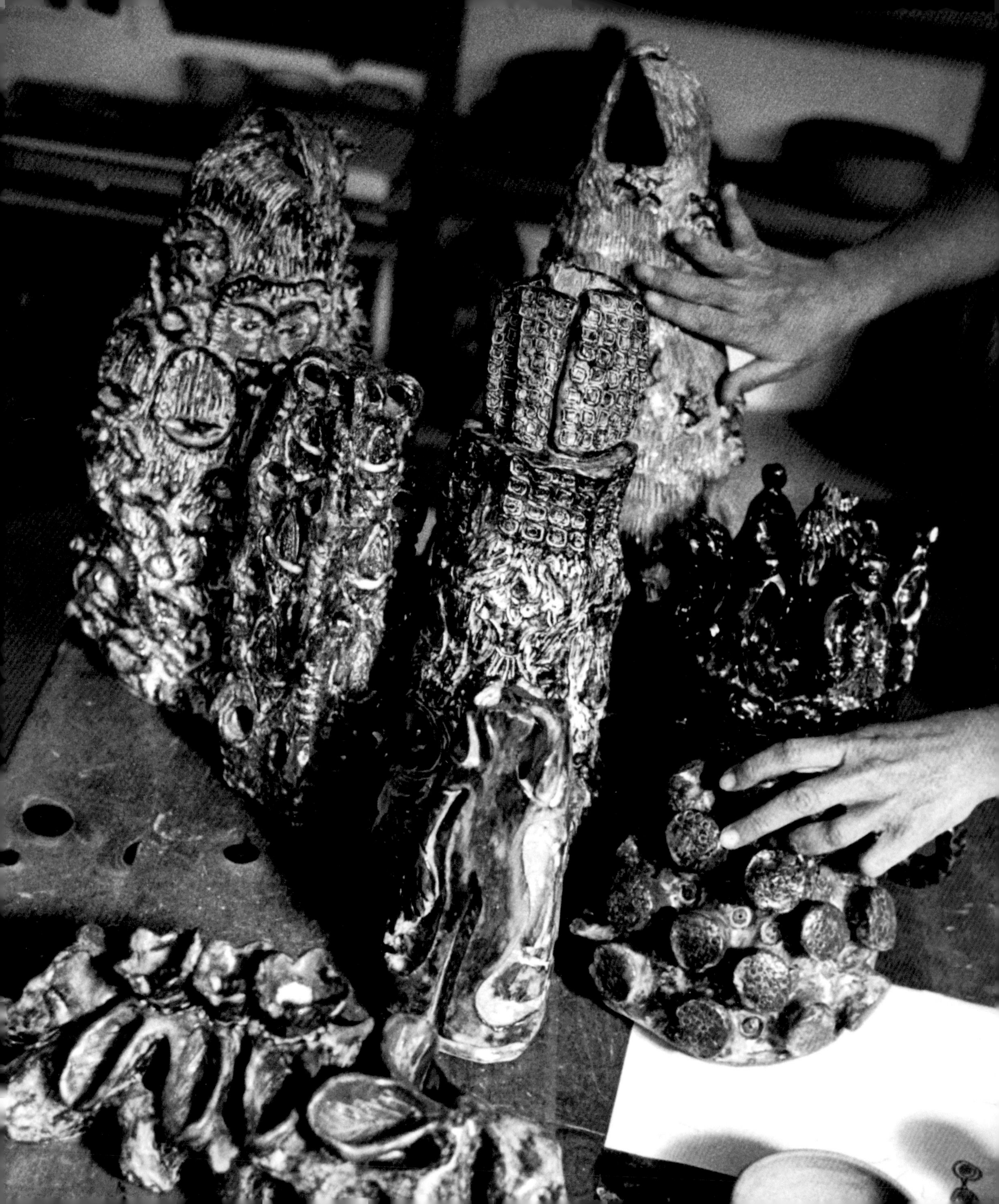

TECLA TOFANO

THIS BODY OF MINE

EDITED BY

GABRIELA RANGEL

LUIS FELIPE FARÍAS S.

James
Cohan

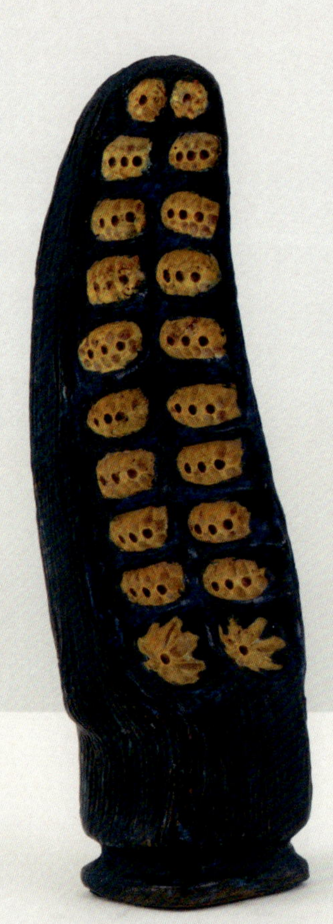
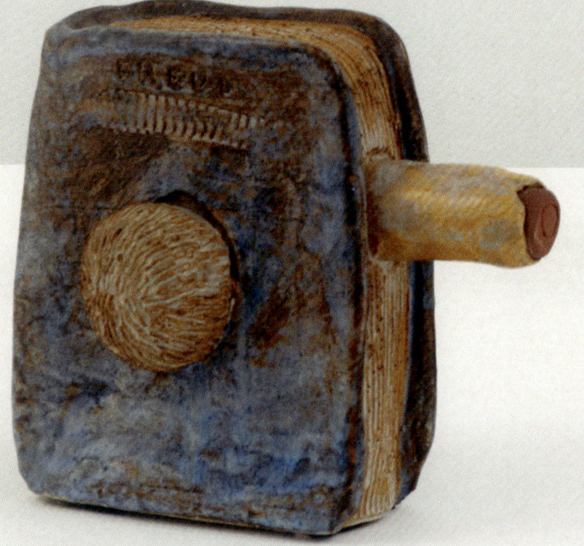

CONTENTS

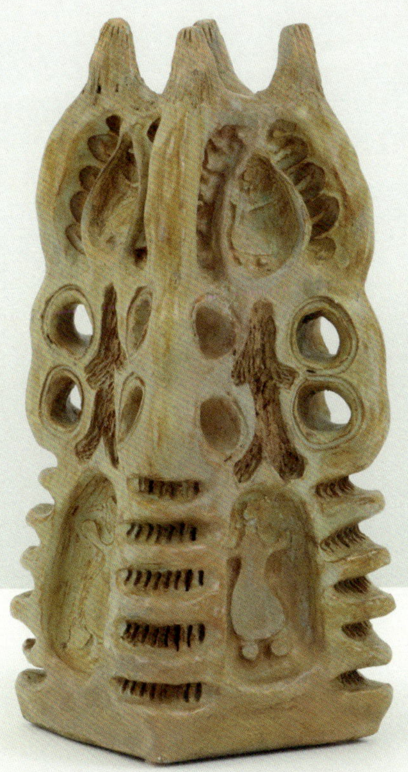

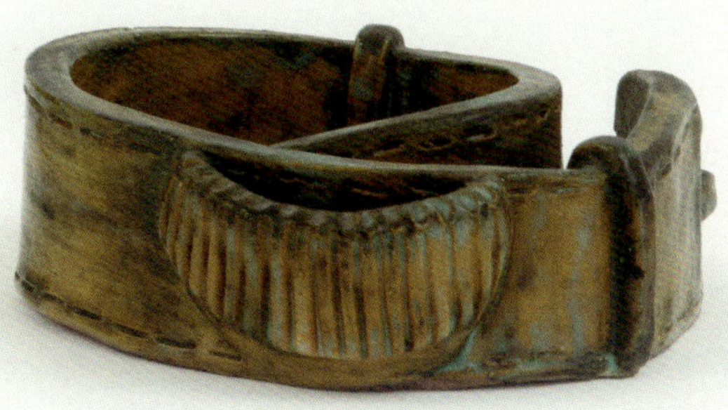

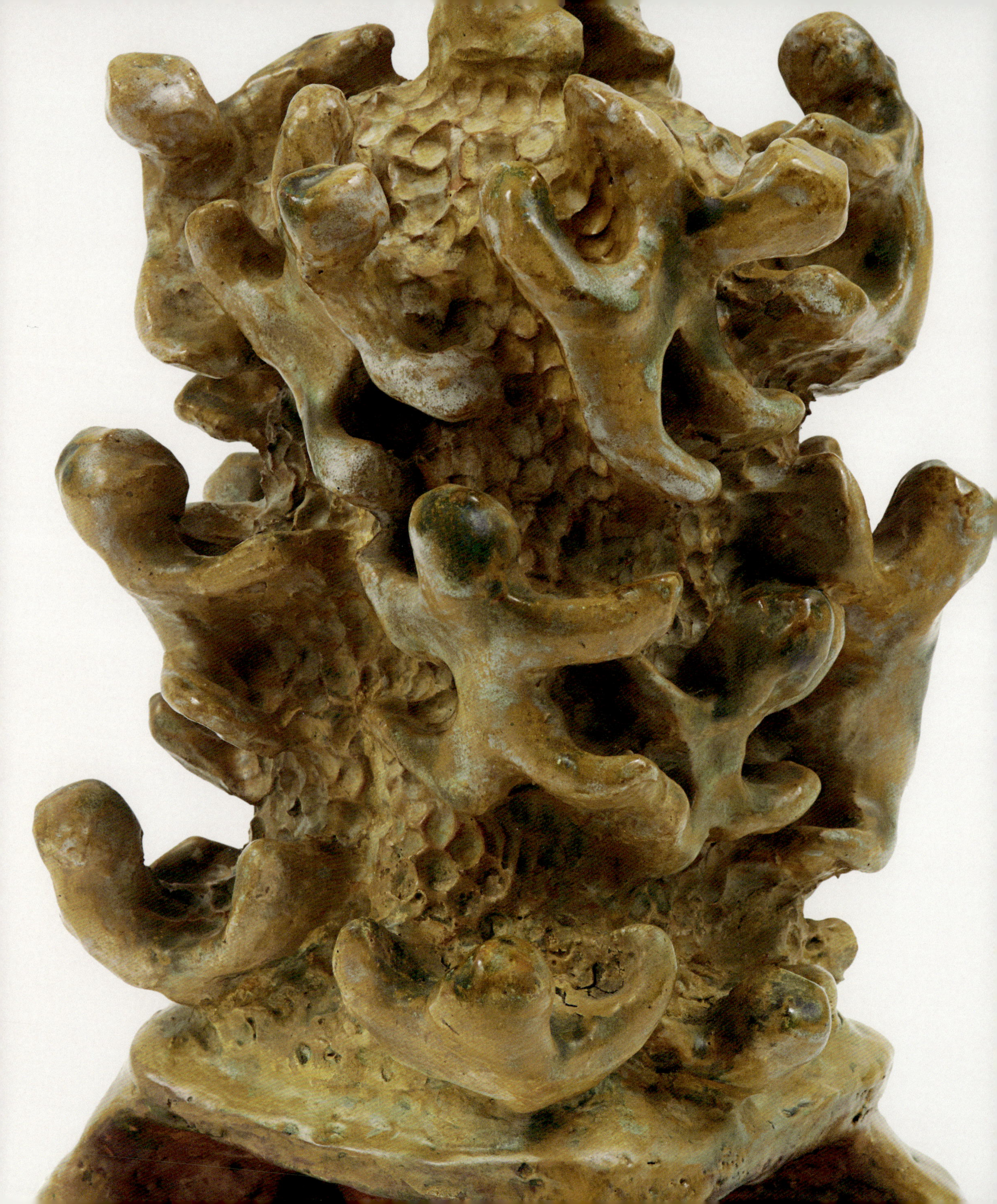

FOREWORD

JAMES COHAN

We are honored to present *Tecla Tofano: This Body of Mine*, the artist's first solo exhibition in the United States. With this exhibition and publication, we aim to shed a brighter light on an artist largely unknown outside of Latin America while exploring her evolution from studio potter to sculptor of deeply affecting imagery.

In her artist statement from 1967, Tofano lamented the inherent lack of mystery in the concentric form of studio pottery and proclaimed her excitement about the potential for more sculptural forms. The ceramic figure, like the golem in Jewish mysticism, is formed from dirt. Its existence speaks to the human desire to create, to seize power, and possibly to offer salvation. The golem embodied every era's dreaded dangers and hopes for redemption. Similarly, Tofano became increasingly aware of an oppressively male-dominated society and boldly used her ceramic forms—and later, her words as a journalist—to address this societal imbalance. This exhibition demonstrates her primal desire to give form to the feminist spirit and to imbue it with a haunting and aesthetic voice. Her work feels deeply personal, and yet it touches upon universal ideas grounded in activism, feminism, and social critique.

I first encountered the ceramics of Tecla Tofano in Cecilia Alemani's 2022 Venice Biennale exhibition *The Milk of Dreams*. This project was the brainchild of the passionate collector Luis Felipe Farías; his critical role in preserving and shaping the historical legacy of Tofano's work is a true gift to future generations. We are deeply indebted to Farías as well as to curator Gabriela Rangel, who has helped give shape to the important narrative arc of Tofano's artistic journey. Audrée Anid is the invaluable linchpin to realizing every facet of this project. As cocurator along with Rangel, it is Anid's commitment to exacting excellence that enabled the exhibition and publication to come to fruition. I would also like to thank Carolina Arnal, Lucía Hinojosa Gaxiola, and Todd Bradway for their work on the publication.

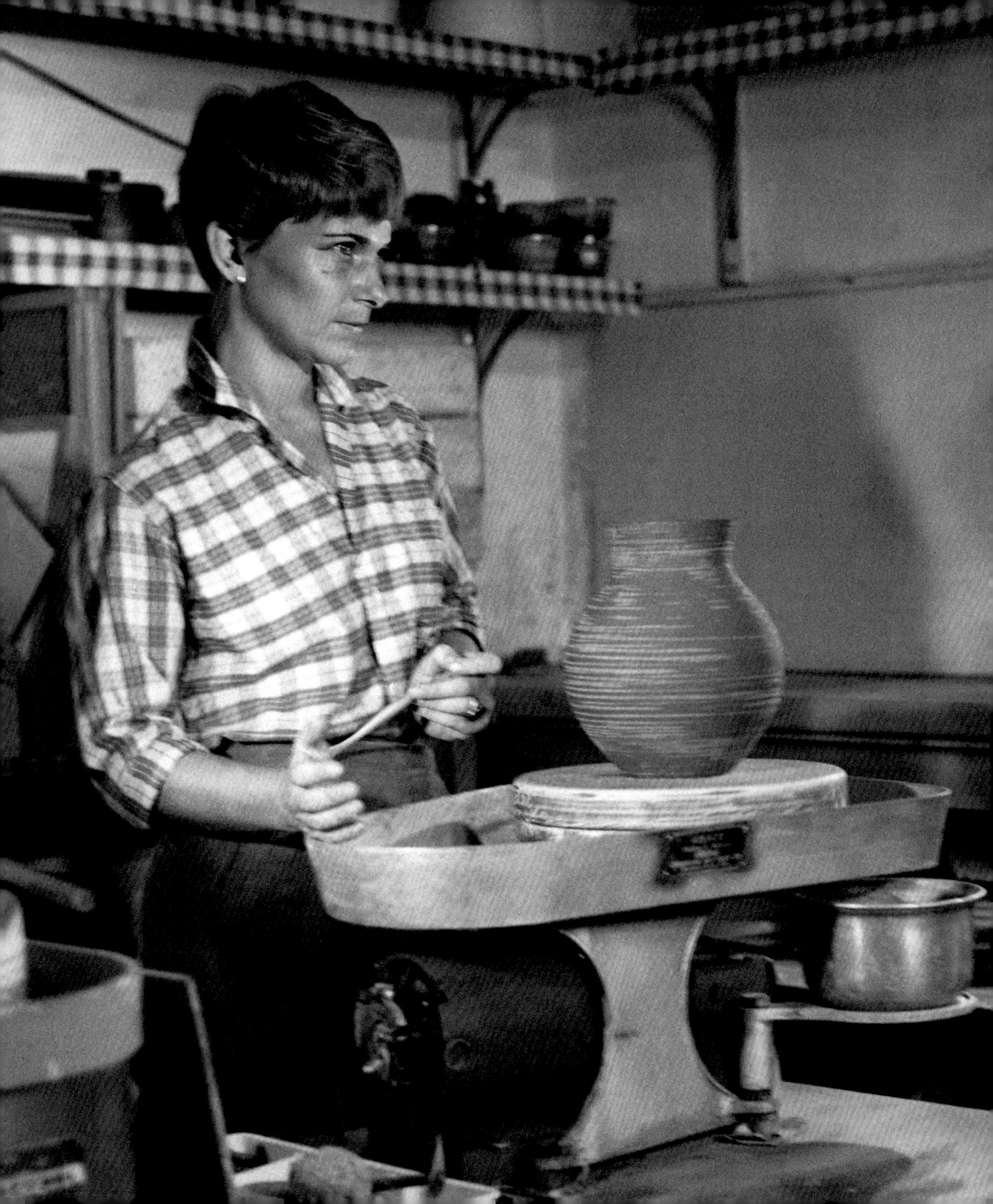

INTRODUCTION

AUDRÉE ANID

A disembodied tongue, a skeletal dragon, creviced totemic towers, and Eve bound by ropes: these visions are a conduit to the imaginative and emotive mind of Tecla Tofano (b. March 5, 1927, in Naples, Italy, d. October 20, 1995, in Caracas, Venezuela). She was an observer, a maker, and a vocal critic who was unafraid of working in opposition to the dominant culture of her time. Tofano channeled her ideas most notably through ceramics, though she was also an adept draftswoman, a metalsmith, and a voracious writer. She utilized her artistic output as an expressive tool to communicate her activist rhetoric, which was directly influenced by public discourse and policy.[1] Her work revealed the cracks in an extremist sociopolitical system in Venezuela, her home of over forty years.

Tofano's meditations in clay were often infused with her biting sense of humor, though they also maintained a poignant and personal undertone. She was heavily enmeshed in the studio craft movement in Caracas. Her initial foray into pottery in the 1950s began with the more traditional approach of throwing utilitarian objects on the wheel. By the 1960s and into the '70s, she shifted to hand-modeling body parts (including genitalia) as well as domestic items ranging from food and books to totemic figures, flora, and fauna. Exhibitions of her work, many of which took place in Caracas, caused what critic Marta Traba deemed a "visual scandal."[2] In 2023, Tofano's ceramics and drawings feel eerily contemporary and more prescient than ever. *Tecla Tofano: This Body of Mine* is a collaborative effort to foreground the artist's lasting impact and to cement her place as a critical figure in the history of feminist art and the broader canon of postwar global modernism.

Unconcerned with crafting pretty objects, Tofano embraced *ugliness*, hand-modeling ceramics that celebrated the grotesque.[3] She eschewed lightness and purity by leaning into heaviness through her choice of predominantly earth-toned glazes.[4] She worked in opposition to a refined geometric abstraction and kineticism that was popular among her peers, and instead embraced rough, hand-built surfaces. According to the artist, her objects "filled with nooks, labyrinths, meanderings, have an *internal mystery* that needs to be unraveled."[5] She imbued her ceramics with a sentient quality, wherein figures emerge and tear their way out of hardened clay. Atop the lid that comprises *Vasija con personaje* (Vessel with Personage, 1969; PP. 42–43), hands claw out and encircle a central figure whose arms are raised in a defiant pose, suggesting at once an expression of frustration and a manifestation of breaking free. In *La mujer en la historia* (Women in History, 1975; P. 67), a female figure steps out of the pages of a book entitled *The History of Men*, physically interrupting the dominant patriarchal historical narrative to interrogate and reclaim it.

In the case of Tecla Tofano, it is impossible to divorce her sociopolitical life from her art, as they were so heavily intertwined. Her left-leaning activist views were a direct response to the volatile dictatorial climate that engulfed Venezuela in the 1950s and to the oil boom of the 1960s and '70s. The sudden influx of oil industry wealth caused an economic chasm in Venezuelan society. Tofano reacted to this shift by creating artworks that were embedded with social commentary and incisive criticism of the newly formed elite. An example is the intricately detailed dead fish on a platter, *Bacalao al limón* (Cod with Lemon, 1973; FIG. 2, PP. 52–53), one of the forty-seven ceramics that comprised her installation *Lo que comen los que comen* (What Those Who Eat Eat, 1973; FIG. 1). This "orgiastic display"—a term coined by the critic Perán Erminy—included elaborate dishes, caviar, desserts, and alcohol. It was a nod to the gluttonous habits of the upper echelons, who were represented by doll-like figures sitting around a table.[6]

The female body is addressed in Tofano's visual art and writing as a retort to repression, an affront to pervasive machismo, and a reflection of the artist's personal traumas.[7] Latin American women artists of the 1960s and '70s were reacting to extreme marginalization and instability.[8] Andrea Giunta—the art historian and one of the curators of the groundbreaking 2017 traveling exhibition *Radical Women: Latin American Art, 1960–1985*, which featured Tofano's work—makes the crucial point that "in the case of Latin America, the relationship between the body and violence is central."[9] This statement rings true in Tofano's work. She transmuted her pain in the aftermath of her rape into the haunting and totemic ceramic *Sin título* (Untitled, 1966; P. 40–41). In this work, four etched, shadowy male bodies wrap around its ribbed form and are flanked by eight female figures who hover above and below them: a manifestation of bodily dissociation. Her commanding ceramic tongue, *Lengua tótem* (Totem Tongue, 1966; P. 38–39), with its strong spinal vein running along its underside, underscores the power of this tool for communication. Here, however, Tofano has severed it from the body and effectively silenced it.

Tofano built her own visual and poetic language that crystallized female gestures and experiences, which is overtly illustrated in her series *Evas al desnudo* (Naked Eves), a suite of forty-four pencil drawings from 1972. The drawing *Así empezó todo* (Thus It All Began; P. 79) is an homage to original sin according to the Christian doctrine: a lone Eve, who is nude and blindfolded, grips a snake that is

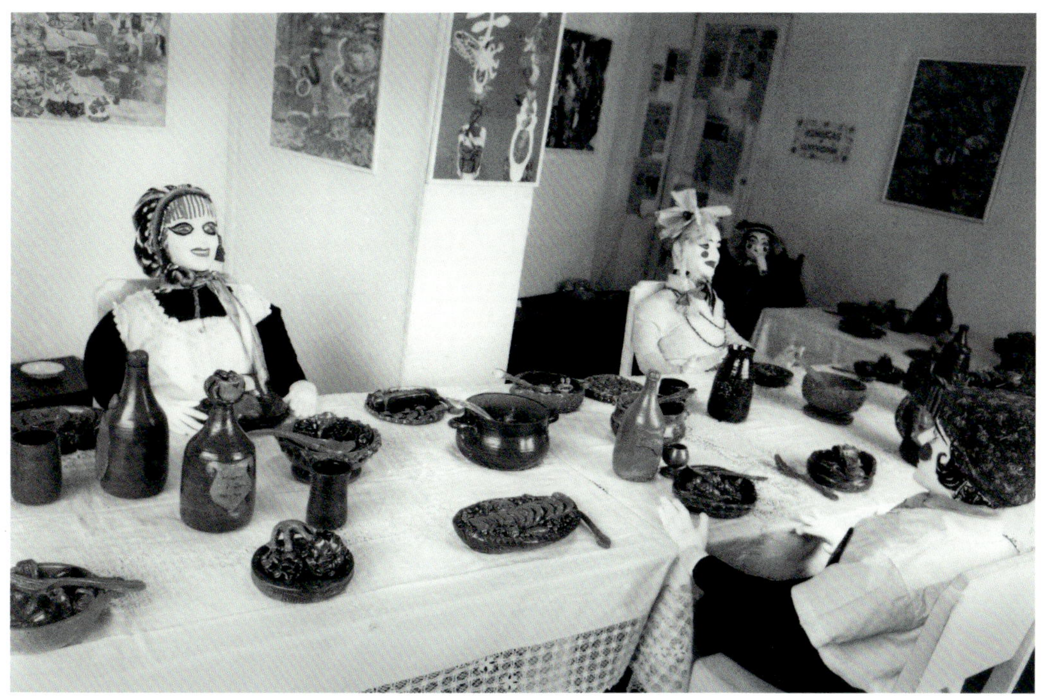

FIG. 1. View of Tecla Tofano's installation *Lo que comen los que comen* (What Those Who Eat Eat), 1973

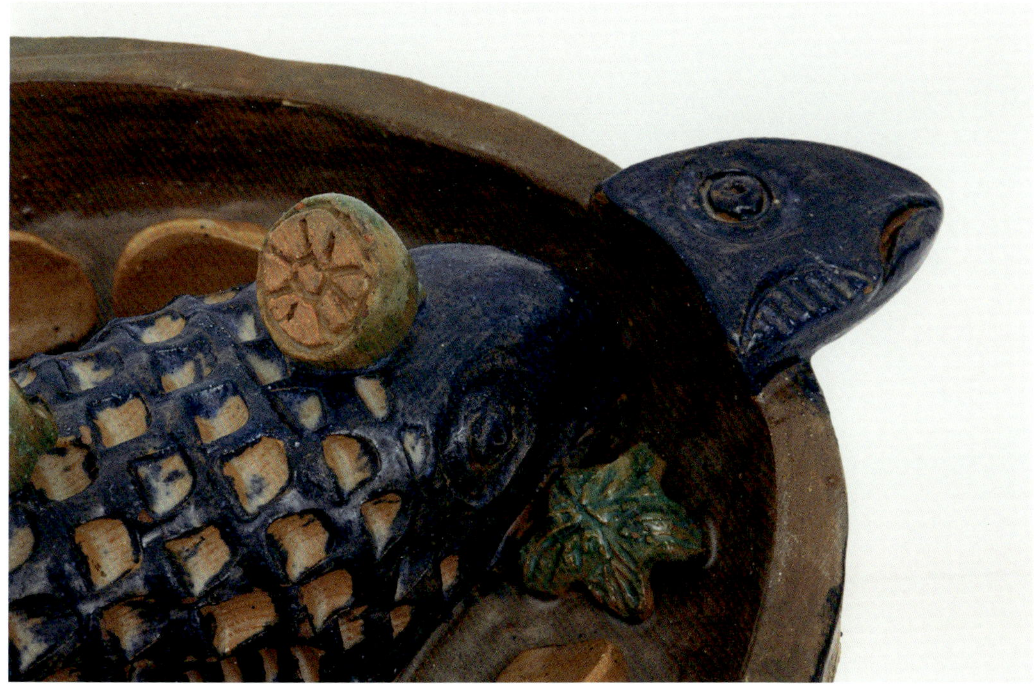

FIG. 2. Tecla Tofano, detail of *Bacalao al limón* (Cod with Lemon), 1973

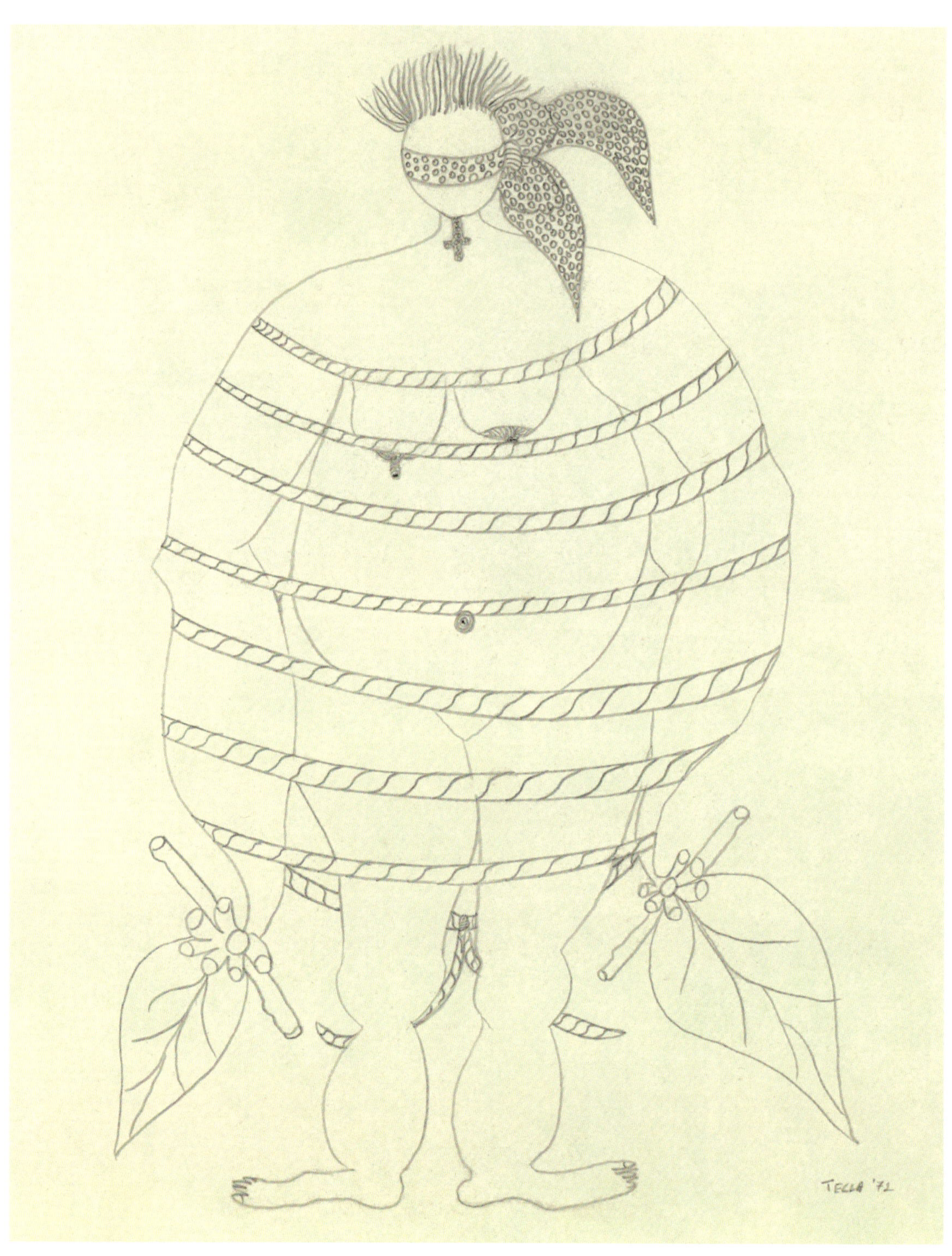

FIG. 3. Tecla Tofano, *Amarrada pero frutal* (Tied but Fruity), from the suite *Evas al desnudo* (Naked Eves), 1972. Pencil on paper; 10⅝ × 8 in. (27 × 21.5 cm)

grazing the forbidden fruit. In Tofano's narrative, Eve, the archetypal woman, is pictured in a multitude of scenarios, from the quotidian to the fantastical. Tofano often made direct references to social stigmas and expectations imposed on women, particularly those involving reproductive and domestic labor. In *Amarrada pero frutal* (Tied but Fruity; FIG. 3), Eve is bound by ropes, which echoes the oppressive confinement of women and the sensation of being trapped.[10] There are obvious references to motherhood in the drawing *Los reproduce* (She Reproduces Them; P. 82), as a shaded figure emerges from a cracked egg, cradled and held by Eve while she teeters on a globe. The imagery recalls the Greek god Atlas, condemned to carry the celestial spheres for eternity. Here, however, Eve carries the enormous responsibility of producing new life. Tofano's ruminations on the body found in her ceramics, drawings, and writings underscore the artist's deeply rooted commitment to expressing the paradoxes of being a woman and to rendering visible what was once considered taboo.

ENDNOTES

1. Gabriele Schor, *The Feminist Avant-Garde of the 1970s: Works from the Sammlung Verbund, Vienna* (Munich: Prestel, 2016), 34.

2. Marta Traba, "Tecla Tofano: Ars Política," *El Nacional*, March 11, 1973, in *Moderno: Design for Living in Brazil, Mexico, and Venezuela, 1940–1978*, eds. Gabriela Rangel et al. (New York: Americas Society, 2015), 220.

3. Cecilia Fajardo-Hill, "Singular Women: Experimental Art in Venezuela," in *Radical Women: Latin American Art, 1960–1985*, eds. Cecilia Fajardo-Hill and Andrea Giunta (Los Angeles: Armand Hammer Museum of Art and Cultural Center, 2017), 308.

4. Traba, "Tecla Tofano," 218.

5. Traba, "Tecla Tofano," 218.

6. Traba, "Tecla Tofano," 218.

7. Amalia Caputo, "Tecla Tofano: A Pioneering Feminist Artist in Venezuela," *Research and Exhibitions Magazine*, Archives of Women Artists, accessed August 1, 2023, https://awarewomenartists.com/en/magazine/tecla-tofano-une-artiste-feministe-pionniere-au-venezuela/.

8. Magalí Arriola, "Pacific Standard Time: South-South," *Frieze*, September 2017, 123.

9. Andrea Giunta, "The Iconographic Turn: The Denormalization of Bodies and Sensibilities in the Work of Latin American Women Artists," in *Radical Women: Latin American Art, 1960–1985*, eds. Cecilia Fajardo-Hill and Andrea Giunta (Los Angeles: Armand Hammer Museum of Art and Cultural Center, 2017), 30.

10. Schor, *The Feminist Avant-Garde*, 41.

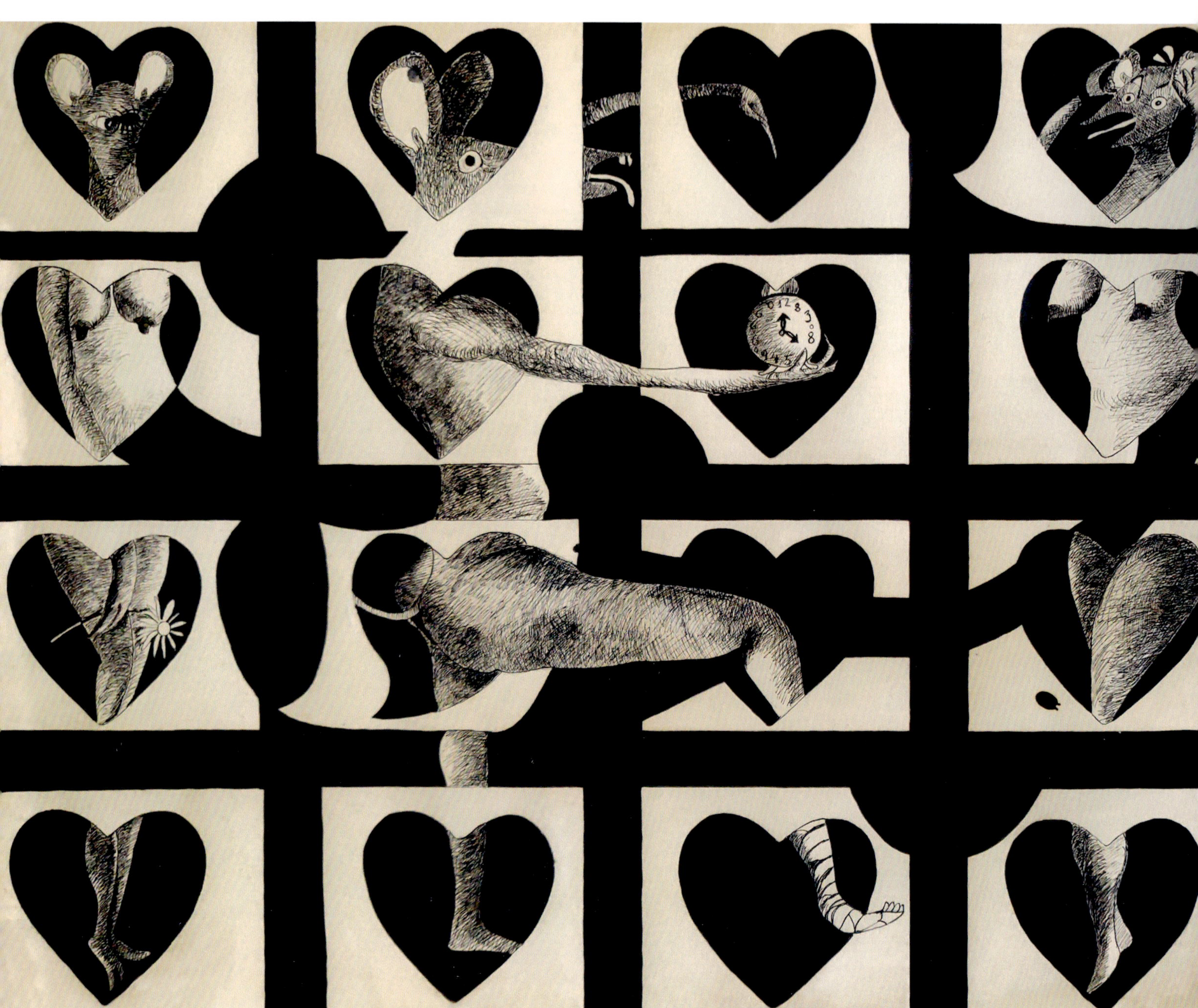

Tecla Tofano, *Sin título* (Untitled), 1967. Ink on cardboard; 20½ × 26⅜ in. (52 × 67 cm)

THIS BODY OF MINE: TECLA TOFANO'S MODELING OF HER WORLD[1]

GABRIELA RANGEL

I can't be free if I don't confront
the separation that should exist between
the past and today. I am. Another one,
rebirth perhaps, I don't depend on anything,
I don't depend on what I was, and
tomorrow I could be another one, I can
remake myself day after day, rebuilt,
to be right, to make a mistake, to fail, but
to live as I am.

TECLA TOFANO, *Yo misma me presento* [2]

A while ago [Tofano's] flowers were expressly
coarse, withered, insolent in their saddened
carnality: however, finally someone
could get something from a bunch of flowers
without being superfluous and puerile.

ROBERTO GUEVARA, *Ver todos los días* [3]

I. THE BIRTH OF A FEMALE PUBLIC INTELLECTUAL

Sometime in the second half of the 1980s, Italian feminist Dacia Maraini visited Caracas to participate in a conference and film screening at the cultural center known as Ateneo de Caracas.[4] Her presence in such a center that attracted the leftist bohemian scene attested to the resonance of European feminism in the country. The crowded event brought together an array of artists, students, liberal professionals, and academic women—among them Tecla Tofano, an energetic artist who often engaged in public polemics in the national press about women's rights. Tofano's intimidating, charismatic, and magnetic presence at the event was palpable, and she was strategically seated close to the speaker in the VIP section of the room, along with other members of the feminist collectives Miércoles and La Mala Vida.[5] During the Q and A session, Maraini and Tofano engaged in a complex discussion about women's autonomy and emancipation—particularly notable in a Catholic country where reproductive rights are still far from secured.[6] In keeping with the activist tone of the discussion, the conference concluded with an admonition to the audience by Tofano: in the immediate future, younger women would need to decide between the phallus and the sewing basket.[7]

The Maraini conference, recorded only in the frail memory of the audience members, reflected the level of public relevance reached by Tofano, whose work engaged feminism through various media. Born in Naples, Italy, in 1927, Tofano migrated to Venezuela in 1952 with her first husband, Armando Córdova, an economist whom she met in Europe.[8] The couple had two children, one of them a daughter who tragically died in a car accident as an infant.[9] When they arrived, the South American country was under the rule of a military regime that was internationally recognized for its substantial investment in public monuments and art philanthropy, as well as its ambition to equal North American and European modernization.[10] In the 1950s, Caracas was a medium-sized city that was adjusting to vast demographic changes: a wave of newcomers had relocated from Venezuela's isolated, agricultural interior, in part to escape the tropical maladies found there, like malaria and Chagas disease.[11] In addition, when Tofano arrived in the capital with no knowledge of Spanish, she encountered a large community of Italian and Spanish immigrants living in both middle- and lower-class neighborhoods that had either been developed specifically for them or transformed upon their arrival. They were part of a wave of European workers and professionals who migrated to Venezuela after the Second World War, responding to the growing need for labor to support infrastructure projects aimed at transforming Caracas into a modern city designed for cars and high-rises.[12] Once settled in this dynamic new community, Tofano enrolled in the art school to study applied arts under the tutelage of Miguel Arroyo—an artist, designer, curator, and critic.

According to Tofano:

I arrived in Venezuela without speaking a single word of Spanish. For that reason, I was troubled about the difficulties that I had to confront to get closer to this people that I felt already like mine [sic]. I aimed to participate actively in some way to feel more integrated to this land. Then, helped by some like Alejandro Otero, Sarita Mendoza, and Miguel Arroyo, I entered to the School of Plastic Arts and Applied Arts in Caracas in 1954, the year when Miguel Arroyo was appointed director of the School of Ceramics. It wasn't much [sic] necessary to achieve a proficiency in the Spanish language to learn craft dictated by the will to learn a practice in which the hands, the body, and the spirit are actively more important than speaking.[13]

Arroyo attracted a coterie of young creative women including Tofano to be part of his ceramic workshop Forma Veinte.[14] With determination and great commitment this outstanding group of artists began to participate in art salons, collectively initiating the use of the language of abstraction within the discipline of the applied arts in Venezuela [FIG. 1].[15] After a few years of apprenticeships and collaborations during a period of harsh economic constraints during which the group was broke and lacked the necessary tools and materials for glazing—according to Tofano's own testimony—their dedication yielded success: ceramics became highly appreciated among the art elite. In 1958, following a gold medal award of excellence that she received at a national salon, Tofano became one of the most distinguished members of the pottery-making circle and a full-time professor at the Universidad Central de Venezuela. Two years later, Arroyo was appointed director of the Museo de Bellas Artes, where pottery was often exhibited in its galleries and permanently displayed and sold at the museum shop.

While it's tempting to only trace a linear account of Tofano's career in order to summarize her ascendance into the elite modernist group of women ceramists in Venezuela, her artistic journey expanded to new directions, too. It's true that she achieved a dazzling career trajectory during the height of pottery making's acceptance and popularity, despite its designation as a minor practice in comparison to the beaux arts. But in the 1960s, Tofano's celebrated work changed significantly, which has prompted historians and critics to divide her career conceptually into two distinct phases based on their underlying artistic approaches and methods.[16] Accordingly, in her early period (1955–63), she produced functional objects and vessels using traditional techniques, including the pottery wheel and different glaze processes [FIG. 2]. After 1964, however, Tofano engaged sociopolitical

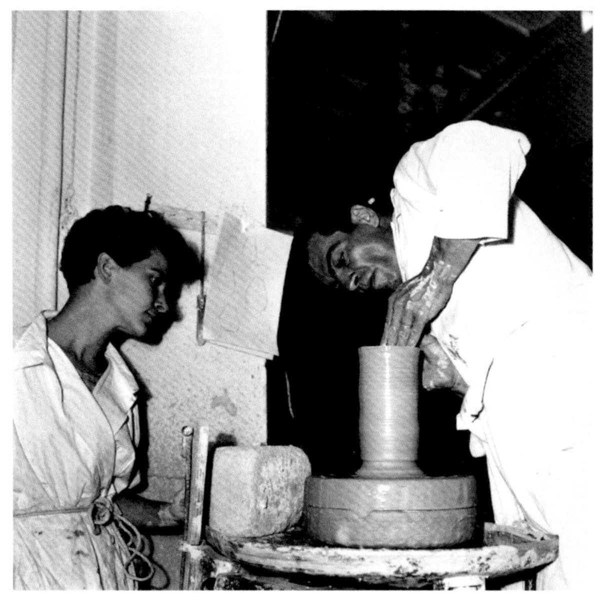

FIG.1. Tecla Tofano and Miguel Arroyo, ca. 1955

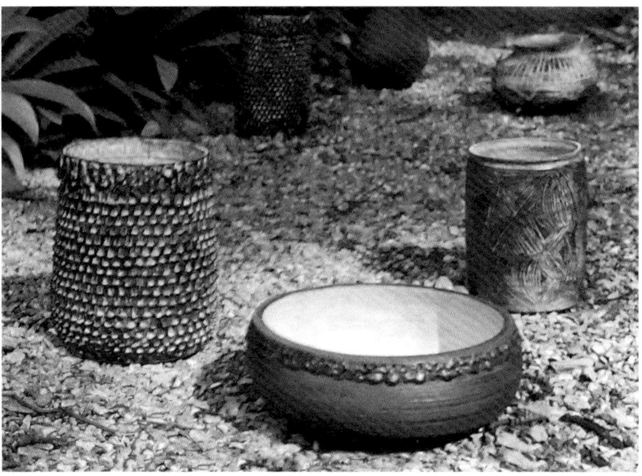

FIG.2. View of Tecla Tofano's exhibition at the Museo de Bellas Artes, Caracas, 1961

discourse through her work, challenging conventional beauty standards as she transitioned to a figurative practice that often blended clay modeling with expressive sculptural techniques. The outstanding work *Vasija con personaje* (Vessel with Personage, 1969; PP. 42–43) attests to Tofano's growing resistance to creating functional objects. The vessel's expressionistic lid—which includes a modeled figure with open arms surrounded by a circle of hands—contradicts its functionality.

Unfortunately, much of Tofano's biography has been systematically wiped out from her work. Significant aspects of her life—such as her adjustment to a new culture, the challenges she faced establishing herself as a professional married woman artist with children, and her two divorces in a conservative society, where she proudly maintained a reputation as a nonconformist until her death—are hardly considered in the existing research, including Marta Traba's in-depth essay about the artist.[17] Tofano's struggle dealing with her position within the clay and fire community as a gendered and formalist practice with no contextual engagement entered into a crisis after she received important awards in Prague in 1961 and Buenos Aires in 1962.[18] It is no coincidence that at that time she started to expand her ceramics practice and also began to teach and to publish—first a children's book dedicated to her son, Daniel, and later regular press articles about culture and politics. In this moment, she emerged as a public intellectual bearing an uncompromising counternarrative to a formalist model of modernity.

II. A POROUS TEXTURE FOR CONCEPTUAL BIFURCATIONS

Tofano's aesthetic shift coincided with the appearance of strong divisions and agitation in Venezuela's political and cultural landscape at the beginning of the 1960s. This period was marked by two military insurrections that created national chaos.[19] At the same time, radical factions of artists, academics, and intellectuals close to the Communist Party and extreme left political forces embraced the fervor and confrontational spirit of the Cuban Revolution and its concomitant rejection of the bourgeois order. The Universidad Central de Venezuela sheltered different cadres of insurgent youth and politically engaged intellectuals who supported the idea of general insurrection, making it the center of the rebellion against the newly elected democratic government of Rómulo Betancourt.[20]

Tofano's inner circle of friends and family was part of the sphere of ideological divergence that was ignited at the Universidad Central.[21] In 1965 she participated in a group show organized by the neo-Dada guerrilla art group El Techo de la Ballena, following a militant period during which she often participated in exhibitions by galleries affiliated with the radical left, like El Pez Dorado, Viva México, and Sala Ocre. Her drawings, which in the early 1960s depicted vernacular fables like *¿Quien inventó la silla?* (Who Invented the Chair?), became a medium for her activism, characterized by scenes of sexual difference that convey gender inequality such as *Seductora* (Seducer; FIG. 3) and *Parirás* (You'll

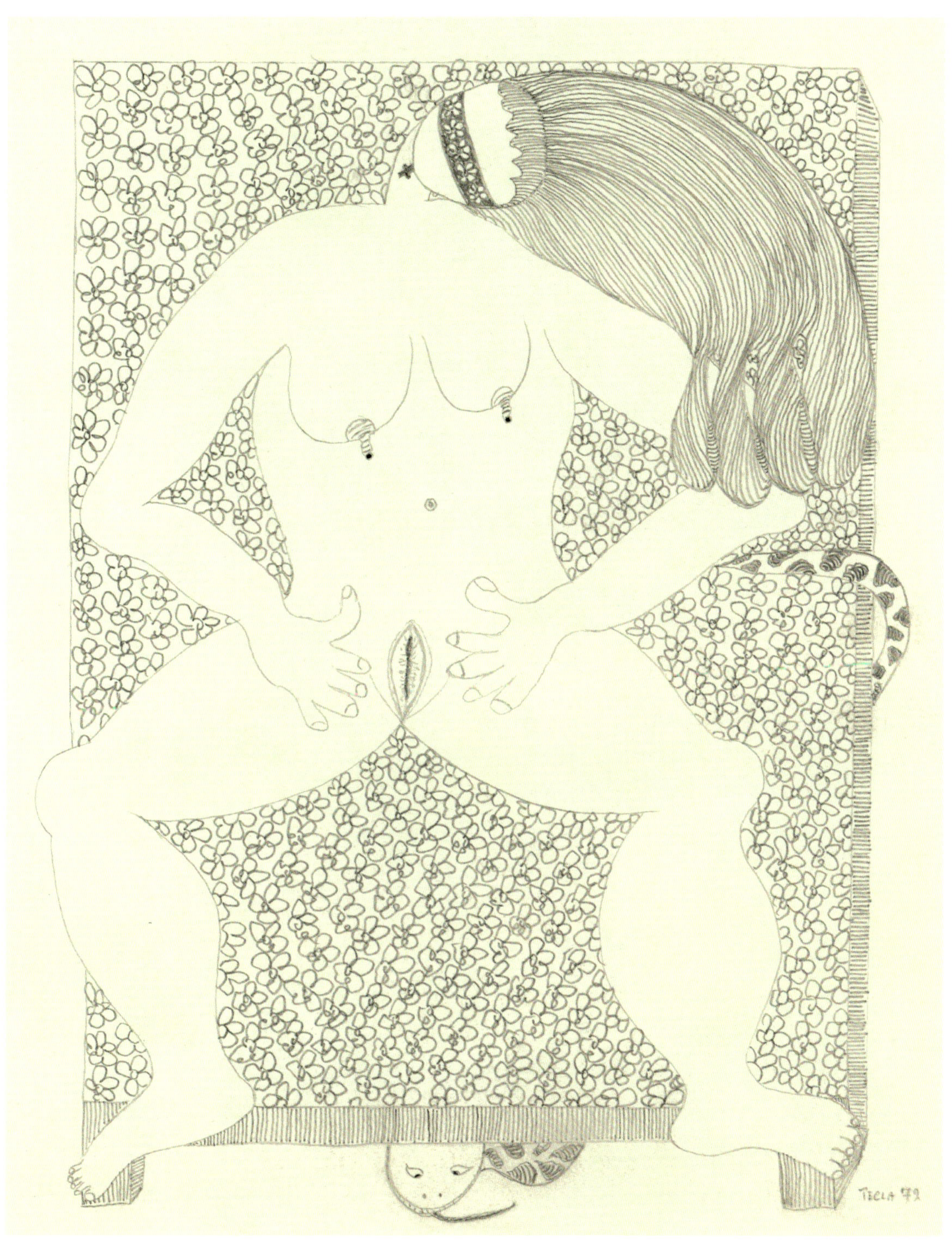

FIG. 3. Tecla Tofano, *Seductora* (Seducer), from the suite *Evas al desnudo* (Naked Eves), 1972. Pencil on paper; 10⅝ × 8 in. (27 × 21.5 cm)

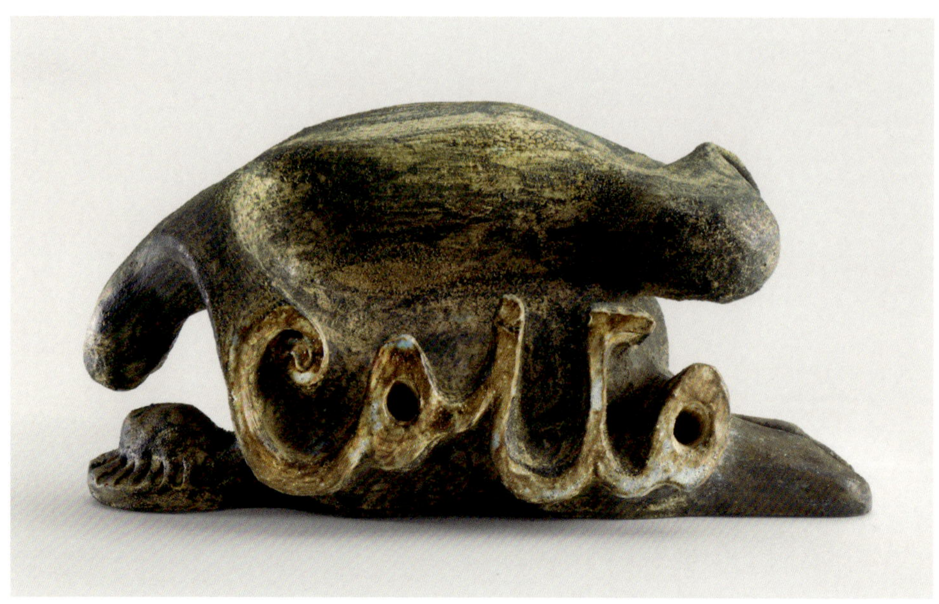

FIG. 4. Tecla Tofano, *Coito* (Coitus) from the series *30 pecados vitales* (30 Vital Sins), 1974.
Clay and enamel; 5 ¼ × 9 ¾ × 4 ½ in. (13.3 × 24.8 × 11.4 cm)

Deliver; P. 75), both from the suite of drawings *Evas al desnudo* (Naked Eves, 1972; PP. 70–84). At the same time, she exhibited individually and in group shows at institutional venues such as the Museo de Bellas Artes and the Sala Mendoza. But how did Tofano's artistic choices change so abruptly?

Critics like Roberto Guevara have implied that while Tofano was part of the Venezuelan distinguished ceramics circle, her vessels did not fully conform to the tenets of abstract beauty and perfection achieved by her most talented peers, like Cristina Merchán, María Luisa de Tovar, Reina Herrera, Josefina Alvarez, or in particular the celebrated Seka Severin de Tudja.[22] Instead, Tofano's utilitarian work featured tough, raw compositional elements that were made through incisions and splits in the clay and uneven textures formed

under glazed surfaces in quotidian objects such as an ashtray (1965) or a tall vase (1961) [P. 34]. The engobe process of her functional vessels evoked what Walter Benjamin described as the chaotic identity of Naples, where sumptuous Baroque buildings show a porous matter pervasively visible on their stones.[23]

Marta Traba considered Tofano to be a singular and outstanding artist in the region, who not only broke down the formalist conventions of Venezuelan modern art but, resisted its docile commodification with oppositional strategies that the critic defined with the latin term *ars politica*.[24] Nonetheless, Traba found problematic Tofano's elaboration of a theoretical apparatus that interpreted her own work. For the critic it created a difficulty for contextualizing the work. Paradoxically, she praised Tofano's ability to express herself through different "systems of communication," recognizing her ability to excel both as a writer of fiction, essays, and poetry and as an artist who made piles of drawings.[25] However, Traba offered a warning about these separate lines of thinking, which in her view were "saying three different things at once," and admonished the artist to choose ceramics as her central practice in order to consolidate and connect her diverse forms of creative expression.

Traba's pragmatic decision to frame Tofano's practice through ceramics didn't solve the incomplete puzzle of the artist's limitless creativity vis-à-vis her position as a public intellectual and a feminist activist—roles that Tofano expressly referenced in her pieces *Objeto/Recompensa* (Object/Reward, 1975; FIG. 6), and *La mujer en la historia* (Women in History, 1975, P. 67) from the series *De género femenino* (Of the Female Gender). The work depicts a modeled figurine of a woman who ironically emerges from a book entitled *Historia del hombre* (The History of Men).[26] Another outstanding work from the series *Los enlatados* (The Canned), *Sin título* (Untitled, 1970; P. 51), merges her critique of capitalist consumerism with a corrosive yet humorous observation about patriarchal repression: a flower and a hand struggle to escape their imprisonment from the domestic realm signified by the square basket that traps them.

Analyzing Tofano's feminist politics only through her ceramics practice highlights societal exclusionary tactics that perpetuated broader inequalities that extended beyond gender. Moreover, entirely disregarding the personal elements within these works also seems to be a limiting approach. Traba's singular focus also indicates her own ideological struggles to understand and accept feminism as a cluster of critical discourses that either celebrated or emancipated an essence—the contested category of "woman." Setting aside Traba's meager analysis in which Tofano's biography was practically erased and her activism minimized, I would argue that it's essential to understand Tofano also as an accomplished intellectual and agitator in order to connect the dots of her creative expression into one axis. Judith Butler asserts the empowering nature of feminism: "The feminist impulse, and I am sure that there is more than one, has often emerged in the recognition that my pain or my silence or my anger or my perception is finally not mine alone, and that it delimits me in a shared cultural situation which in turn enables and empowers me in certain unanticipated ways."[27] In a similar vein, it's clear that for Tofano the feminist impulse empowered her to examine, in both her art and writing, the female body as a tactical space of confrontation.

For Tofano and a few other women in her circle, the body was the conduit for formulating an equal status for women and the ultimate space—rather than object—employed to transform the patriarchal society. It is not accidental that Tofano's first book, composed of short stories and drawings for children, is entitled *¿Quien inventó la silla?* (Who Invented the Chair?) Furthermore, she was reluctant to define her clay practice in teleological terms, preferring instead to situate it conceptually between sculpture and ceramics, craft and art, functional and nonfunctional—a common move among other outstanding women artists in Venezuela at the time. For example, a similar discomfort with being part of the Western art historical canon prompted Gego to reject the definition of sculpture for her three-dimensional wire meshes and reticular structures and motivated Elsa Gramcko to define her totems as painted sculptures and her assemblages as eyes. Tofano's conceptual development of her ceramics exposed the traditional canon and its critical vocabulary as patriarchal and reductionist. This critical aim was theoretically incorporated into the introduction to the Sala Mendoza exhibition *De la silla a la cápsula* (From the Chair to the Capsule), presented in 1969. What is a chair but a negative space, an absent body?

III. DISMANTLING THE VERTEBRAE OF HER TIME

During Tofano's radical years after 1966, she systematically scrutinized the body as the nucleus for exploring poetic and political concerns. In a series of modeled and thematic ceramics, she presented a panoply of interconnected themes: clothing (*Los accesorios*), class (*Lo que comen los que comen* and *30 pecados vitales*; FIG. 4), and gender construction and sexual difference (*De género femenino, Esa Munda Macha, Del libro y su evasión, Las señoras,* and *Ella, él … ellos*). This interrelated approach is also developed in her poetry book *Epílogos* (Epilogues, 1987).

The drawings series *Evas al desnudo* (Naked Eves; PP. 70–84) created an in-depth examination of different forms of power and male domination as well.[28]

At the beginning of the 1960s, Tofano's ceramic work aimed to center the body, whereas local canonical abstract artists erased it. Her first attempts to bring a wide range of body-related topics to her ceramics were filled with totems (tongues) and indigenous weaving motifs—visual strategies common to modern art and aligned with the research promoted by her earlier mentor Miguel Arroyo, who studied the clay practices of preconquest Venezuelan communities. In the next two decades, Tofano's three-dimensional work, drawings, and writing examined different aspects of bodily explorations by focusing on flowers, phalluses, and domestic interiors. Simultaneously, she publicly opposed the reductionism of dyads like privilege-discrimination, visibility-invisibility, abstract-figurative, and female-male. This prompted her to propose a fluid, nonbinary element through the discourses of sexuality and gender.[29] Her uncensored visions are autobiographical and can be compared to the expressive and sexualized work of the self-taught artist Carol Rama (Torino, 1918–2015), who also experimented with different media and materials to explore the fantasies, fears, and violence of intimacy.[30]

In Tofano's ruminations about her practice, her refusal to equate her ceramics to sculpture redirected her to take a closer look at the properties of modeling: "Modeling is not new in the history of ceramics. I believe that modeling is not always

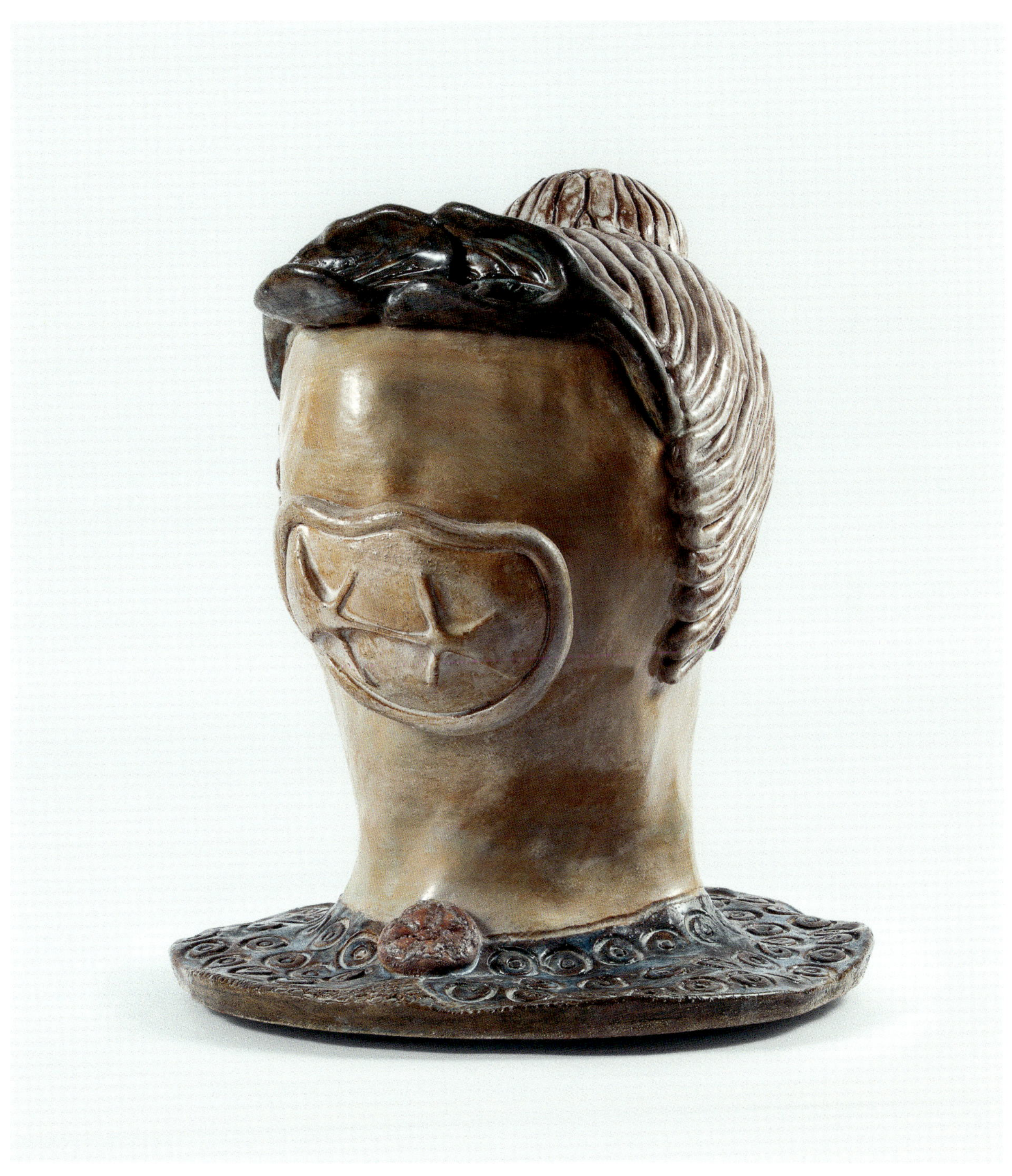

FIG. 5. Tecla Tofano, *Señora Gloriosa de Virtud* (Mrs. Glorious of Virtue), from the series *Las señoras* (Ladies), 1976. Glazed ceramic; 10 ⅝ × 7 ½ × 6 ¾ in. (27 × 19 × 17 cm)

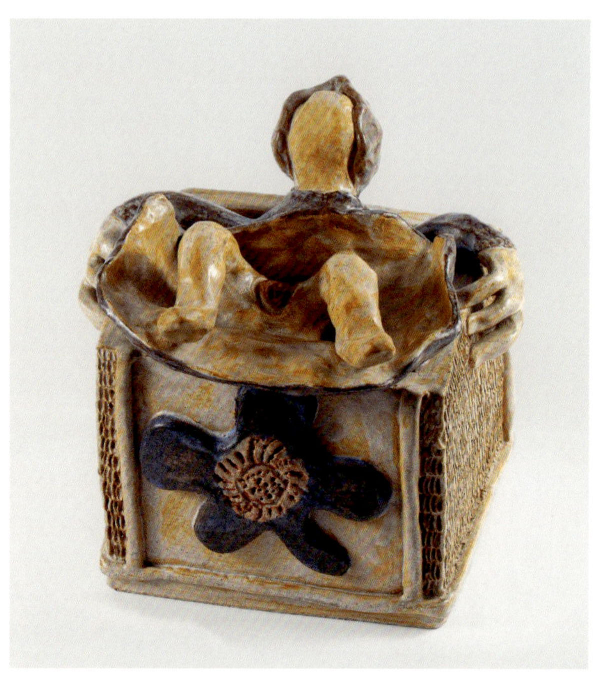

FIG.6. Tecla Tofano, *Objeto/Recompensa* (Object/Reward), from the series *De género femenino* (Of the Female Gender), 1975. Glazed ceramic; 8 ¼ × 7 ⅛ × 9 in. (21 × 18 × 23 cm)

sculpture if we agreed that its aim is to fathom the nature of its matter and limitations and that it should not create authorial limits."[31] In her critical writings, she also referred to her hands as powerful tools that the mind and knowledge can't parallel: "My hands do what my mind and knowledge can't make it or contribute with because they don't have hands."[32] Perhaps her change of direction from the abstract to the figurative in her exploration of the physical nature of ceramics prompted her to write the introspective autobiographical fiction *Yo misma me presento* (I Introduce Myself). In this book, the omniscient narrator is a woman whose coming-of-age exploration of her sexuality and gender begins in Europe,

presumably in Naples, and ends with metaphysical musings about pleasure and pain as reflected in multiple images and soliloquies. The work *Ella, él… ellos* (She, He… They, 1977; FIG.7), which belongs to the collection of the Galería de Arte Nacional in Caracas, consists of three figures made in clay whose limbs are separated from their bodies. Each figure embodies the notion of sexual difference: the female figure has breasts and is pregnant; the male figure's genitals are covered by an Adamic leaf; and the third figure has both male and female genitalia. For Tofano, this third figure represented the end of the era of patriarchal division of labor with the presence of two small figures suckling each nipple.[33] Though breastfeeding is biologically a female capability, Tofano defies this norm by creating a nonbinary figure who impartially provides milk to two infants, transcending sexual distinctions. This third figure, and its breastfeeding figurines, revisits and reinvents the iconography of the classical hermaphrodite, as Amalia Caputo has pointed out. Overall, *Ella, él. . . ellos*, which belongs to the last series made by Tofano, is pivotal in her oeuvre, as the artist announced her retirement from the "red clay practice" after completing it.

Tofano's body-focused approach to modeling in ceramics led her to the development of a pioneering intersectional approach. In fact, Tofano's different creative paths allowed her to interconnect class discrimination and racial and gender inequality through her position as a public intellectual-activist-artist. She did so by drawing from discussions about how to dismantle the patriarchy by using categories created by such a structure of domination debated between international feminist theorists like Julia Kristeva, Luce Irigaray, and Judith Butler and in dialogue with her Venezuelan feminist peers of the Grupo Feminista Miércoles (Feminist Group Miércoles) and its cornerstone Mujeres al Socialismo.

Intersectionality also seems to be correlated to Tofano's exploration of the body through different media, as in *Yo misma me presento,* which journeys through the process of constructing a female subjectivity that runs independently from, or in spite of, logocentric male structures.[34] Her ceramics, drawings, and writing propelled the artist in a direction that Giorgio Agamben defines as "contemporary." In 1987 Tofano discussed the ideological contradictions of a hate crime against a lesbian couple who were celebrating their commitment ceremony at a gay bar when a policeman brutally killed one of them.[35] Her analysis of the murder examined the class and race of the victim, the couple's legal dispossession, and the lack of empathy of the local intellectual elite, as demonstrated by the celebrated queer writer who published a frivolous satire about the circumstances of the crime and the blatant bigotry of a theater critic. Her arguments showed how the so-called enlightened local elite was a part of the discriminatory system and its associated social structures that made the case an emblematic and tragic example of classism, racism, and LGBTQ discrimination.

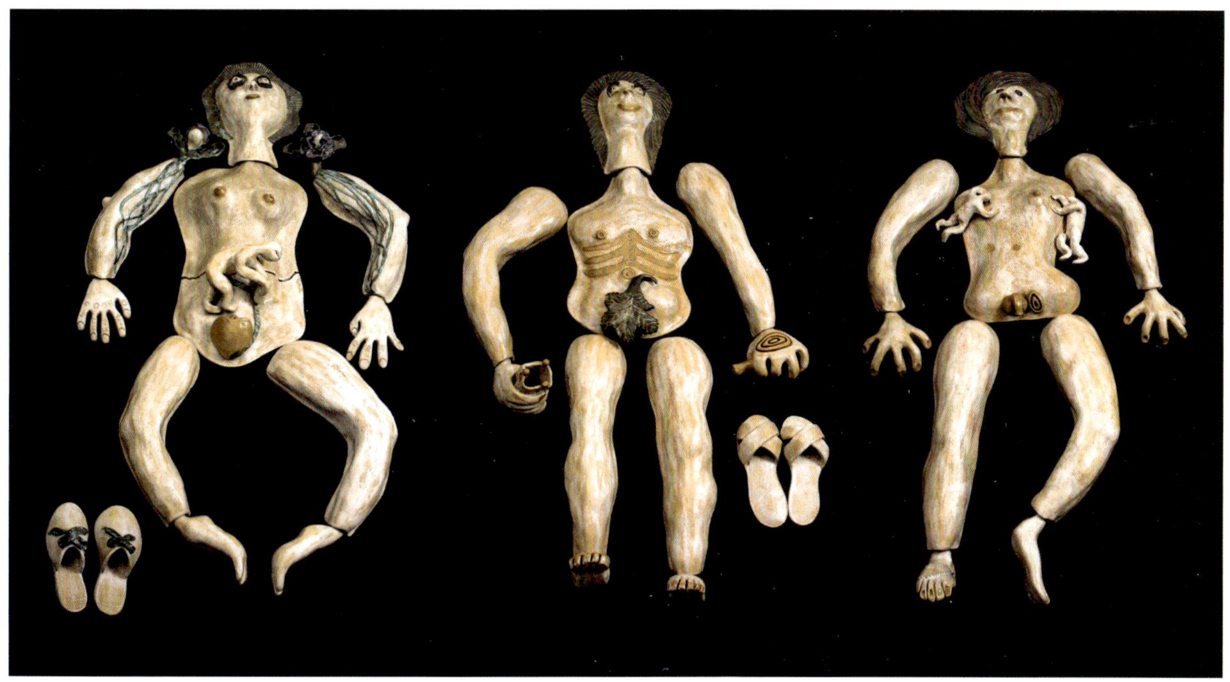

FIG. 7. Tecla Tofano, *Ella, él. . . ellos* (She, He… They), 1977. Glazed ceramic; variable dimensions

Presentness is a temporal notion attached to Agamben's concept of the contemporary, which he defined as an intentional displacement or a delay of action in relation to the present as if the here and now, which is an elusive time, has not arrived yet.[36] One of the aphoristic passages in which Agamben outlines the notion of contemporaneity is dedicated to examining the unfathomable temporality of fashion as a theological marker in the West, in which to be fashionable is to be displaced in time. A fundamental aspect in Tofano's later works is clothing. For Tofano, clothing accessories in ceramics functioned as intersectional signifiers of gender, sex, or class, in that a shoe or a belt are not represented as mere relics, but as markers of *presentness*—as in her 1971 ceramic work entitled *Cuando me levanto* (When I Wake Up, 1971; P. 62), from her series *Los acessorios* (The Acessories), in which a socked male foot wears a sandal as satire of a quotidian scene that could depict the present. Clothing appears in her ceramics and drawings as an elusive skin of its time, as in *Ella, él … ellos*, in which the shoes lying next to the figures are separate parts of ensembles that suggest gender fluidity.

Perhaps Tecla Tofano's greatest contribution to contemporary art is her eloquent and unique voice disseminated through different creative paths through which she dismantled the vertebrae of her time. Her groundbreaking ceramics, drawings, writing, and activism functioned together as a system to uncover the anomaly of her time, bringing together diverse fragments of temporalities and generations.

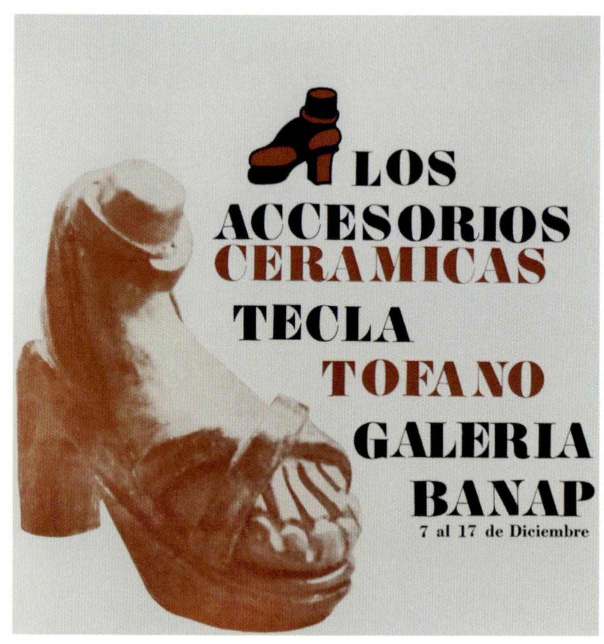

FIG. 8. Cover of the catalogue for *Los accesorios* (The Accessories), Galería Banap, Caracas, 1971

NOTES

1. I want to thank Sagrario Berti for her generous support and for sharing her archive and genuine scholarly interest in Tecla Tofano's work two decades ago. I also want to extend my gratitude to Luis Felipe Farías, whose passion and connoisseurship in the field of ceramics has been key to preserving the history of the practice in Venezuela, in particular that of women artists. I want to also acknowledge James Cohan and Audrée Anid for their support of this project.

2. "No podré ser libre si no logro aceptar la separación que debe existir entre el pasado y el hoy. Soy. Otra, nueva tal vez, no dependo de nada, no dependo de lo que fui, y mañana podría ser otra, puedo rehacerme día a día, reconstruirme, estar en lo cierto, equivocarme, fallar, pero vivir en cuanto soy." Tecla Tofano, *Yo misma me presento* (Caracas: Editorial La Avispa, 1974), 145. Unless otherwise noted, all translations are my own.

3. "Antes sus flores eran expresamente toscas, mustias, insolentes en su carnalidad triste: pero, por fin alguien había podido sacar algo de un manojo de flores que no fuera superfluo y pueril." Roberto Guevara, *Ver todos los días* (Caracas: Monte Ávila Editores, 1981), 160.

4. A recognized public intellectual, Maraini was married to Alberto Moravia, with whom she founded the alternative theater company Il Porcospino. Maraini is still active and recently wrote a book about her friend Pier Paolo Pasolini, *Caro Pier Paolo* (Milan: Neri Pozza Editore, 2022).

5. Tofano was a member of Grupo Feminista Miércoles (Feminist Group Miércoles), founded in 1977 as a feminist think tank that included photographer Franca Donda, film critic and historian Ambretta Marrosu, and psychoanalyst Gioconda Espina, among other women. La Mala Vida was an activist group that drew more confrontational figures, like Giovanna Mérola who wrote a polemical book about the right to abortion in Venezuela in 1979, edited by the Ateneo de Caracas. These Italian-born feminists made a significant contribution to civil and women's rights in Venezuela.

6. In 1982 a partial reform of the civil code was approved, granting equal legal rights to women. Some members of Tofano's feminist circle took part in the process. Abortion is still forbidden in Venezuela, as in many other nations in Latin America, due to the influence of the Catholic Church and more recently to evangelical churches.

7. As I was part of the audience, I recorded Tofano's eccentric admonition in my journal.

8. Tofano migrated to Venezuela more than a decade after Gertrud Goldschmidt (known as Gego), who was part of the German-Jewish diaspora.

9. Amalia Caputo provided important details about Tofano's marriage and her affiliation with the Italian Communist Party. Amalia Caputo, "'Florece donde te plantaron.' Tecla Tofano, artista pionera del feminismo en Venezuela," Trópico Absoluto, June 17, 2023, https://tropicoabsoluto.com/2023/06/17/florece-donde-te-plantaron-tecla-tofano-artista-pionera-del-feminismo-en-venezuela/. Caputo's article connects Tofano's practice to her biography.

10. Lisa Blackmore aptly named the years of the military junta and the Marcos Pérez Jiménez regime in Venezuela "spectacular modernity." Lisa Blackmore, *Spectacular Modernity: Dictatorship, Space, and Visuality in Venezuela, 1948–1958* (Pittsburgh: University of Pittsburgh Press, 2017).

11. Surrealist artist Remedios Varo spent a short period of time in Maracay (1948–50), a provincial city where her brother and family were based. Varo's brother was working on the anti-malaria division created years before to eradicate the tropical disease. I owe this valuable information to Norah Horna, who runs her mother's archive in Mexico City.

12. Historian Fernando Coronil observed: "After the second world war, when Europe was in ruins, Venezuela went through an oil peak due to the increase of the international trade and commerce. Between

1944 and 1950 the oil industry duplicated the local oil production from 700,000 to 1,500,000 barrels per day. The European residents in Venezuela—fundamentally Spanish and Italian—spread the rumor amongst their relatives and friends that 'in Venezuela money runs in the streets.'" Fernando Coronil, *El Estado Mágico, Naturaleza, dinero y modernidad en Venezuela* (Caracas: Nueva Sociedad y Consejo de Desarrollo Científico de la Universidad Central de Venezuela, 2002), 368.

13. Tecla Tofano, "Ceramista Venezolana", *Punto*, September 1963. Centro de Información y Documentación Nacional de las Artes Plásticas (CINAP) at the Galeria de Arte Nacional, Caracas. The original Spanish text reads: "Llegué a Venezuela sin conocer una palabra de español. Por tal motivo me mortificaban las dificultades que tenía para acercarme a este pueblo, que sentía ya como mío. Me propuse participar activamente en alguna forma y sentirme más unida a esta tierra. Ayudada, entonces por aligo como Alejandro Otero, Sarita Mendoza y Miguel Arroyo ingresé a la Escuela de Artes Plásticas y Artes Aplicadas de Caracas en 1954, año en el que Miguel Arroyo iba a dirigir la escuela de cerámica. No se me hacía necesario saber mucho del idioma castellano en ese aprendizaje de artesanía, donde más necesario que el habla era la voluntad de aprender un oficio en el cual las manos, el cuerpo y el espíritu eran lo más activamente importantes."

14. A modernist polymath, Arroyo (1920–2004) studied industrial and applied arts at the Carnegie Institute of Technology in Pittsburgh between 1946 and 1948. In 1949, he opened the Gato store in partnership with artist Alberto Brandt and American expat architect Charles Sink. Lourdes Blanco, "Miguel Arroyo and Pottery," in *Moderno: Design for Living in Brazil, Mexico, and Venezuela, 1940–1978*, eds. G. Rangel and J. Rivas (New York: Americas Society, 2015), 34–36. Arroyo was also part of the group that launched *Los disidentes* magazine (1950) in Paris. The magazine used avant-garde strategies to attack the art establishment in Caracas and to promote geometric abstraction as an ideology of progress and emancipation for the arts.

15. The group also included Cristina Merchán, Seka Severin de Tudja, Reina Herrera, and María Luisa de Tovar.

16. I am referring fundamentally to the Argentine-Colombian critic Marta Traba, who lived in Caracas between 1974 and 1978.

17. Like Gego, Tofano was hired as a full-time professor at the Faculty of Architecture at the Universidad Central de Venezuela, where she taught artistic expression until retirement. Her academic position allowed her some degree of artistic freedom. Tecla Tofano, "Ceramista Venezolana", *Punto*, September 1963. Centro de Información y Documentación Nacional de las Artes Plásticas (CINAP) at the Galeria de Arte Nacional, Caracas. Esmeralda Niño and Alejandro Salas, eds., *Diccionario biográfico de las artes visuales en Venezuela* (Caracas: Galería de Arte Nacional, 2005), 1294–95; and Marta Traba, "Tecla Tofano: Ars Politica," in *Mirar en Caracas* (Caracas: Monte Avila Editores, 1974), 39–50. I will refer to the English translation of Traba's essay in Rangel and Rivas, *Moderno: Design for Living*, 217–222.

18. Ceramics was a practice dominated by women in Venezuela, most of them supposedly coming from well-to-do origins, although Tofano's earlier quoted testimony contradicts this assumption.

19. In 1962 El Porteñazo and El Carupanazo were both failed insurrections against the government that were organized in Puerto Cabello and Carúpano by radical leftist groups in conjunction with military cadres.

20. This eventually led to the emergence of urban guerrillas who persisted until the 1970s.

21. Tecla Tofano married her second husband, Alfredo Chacón, in 1962. The couple had two children and remained together until 1975. A leftist sociologist, Chacón wrote an influential chronicle about the radical period, *La izquierda cultural de Venezuela, 1958–1968*, (Caracas: Editorial Domingo Fuentes, 1970).

22. The critic also described Tofano as a great observer of quotidian occurrences and a critic of consuming society after the emergence of pop art. Guevara, *Ver todos los días*, 159–61. In an earlier article, Guevara stated that her formalist work anticipated her figurative work.

23. "Come la pietra, cosi anche l'architettura di Napoli é porosa. Construzione e azione si permeano in un susseguirsi di cortile, portici e scaloni. Tutto é fatto per custodiare la scena in cui constellazioni sempre nuove, sino ad allora imprevedibili, possano accadere." Walter Benjamin, *Napoli Porosa*, trans. Elenio Cicchini (Napoli: Librería Dante & Descartes, 2020), 16.

24. Marta Traba*, Mirar en Caracas*, 39–50. The critic also described Tofano as a great observer of the quotidian occurrences and a critic of consuming society after the emergence of Pop Art. See: Roberto Guevara, *Ver todos los días* (Caracas: Monte Avila Editores, 1981), 159–161.

25. Marta Traba*, Mirar en Caracas*, 39–50.

26. *La mujer en la historia* (Women in History) depicts a book made of modeled red clay, whose cover reads *Historia del hombre* (The History of Men). A female figurine emerges from the book with her arms wide open holding it. The work conveys the existing contradiction between the book's content and the woman's birth, describing a complicated bond of dependency between sexes: the book as a symbol of knowledge and the woman as an entity produced and (in)formed by men.

27. Judith Butler, "Performative Acts and Gender Constitution," in *The Feminist and Visual Culture Reader*, ed. Amelia Jones (New York: Routledge, 2003), 395.

28. Tofano feminized the masculine words *mundo macho* (macho world) as *munda macha*, disrupting the constitutive gender of the Spanish language, which enables patriarchal dominance of the plural form. By subverting the language's normative gender, she underscored the essential problem of an already sexualized structure.

Therefore, *Esa munda macha* is a title that's impossible to translate into English, a language with practically no gender.

29. The third element uses the mythological example of the hermaphrodite as a remedy to the maladies of biological and ontological debates of sexual difference. Tofano, *Yo misma me presento*.

30. Curiously enough, both artists also made series dedicated to the tarot.

31. "No es nuevo el modelado en la historia de la cerámica. Sostengo que no es escultura siempre y cuando el objetivo se contenga en la problemática de su materia y sus limitaciones y que no debe ser una privación para el autor." Tecla Tofano, "Testimonio de artistas," *Revista Nacional de Cultura* (Caracas, 1967).

32. "Mis manos dan lo que mi cuerpo, mi mente y conocimientos no podrían hacer o dar por no tener dedos." Tecla Tofano, "Reflections," Artist's testimony, *Revista Nacional de Cultura* (Caracas, 1967).

33. Caputo, "'Florece donde te plantaron.'" Caputo quoted literally the artist statement from the exhibition catalogue *Ella, él . . . ellos.* Today, the hermaphrodite, a figure from the classical literature that has both female and male reproductive organs, is questioned by LGBTQ global communities, which uses instead the biological term intersex.

34. In 1971 she received recognition in the José Rafael Pocaterra Literary Award at the Universidad de Carabobo, Valencia, Venezuela. I believe this manuscript mutated into *Yo misma me presento*.

35. Tecla Tofano, "Adónde vamos," *El Nacional*, January 14, 1987.

36. Giorgio Agamben, "¿Qué es lo contemporáneo?," in *Desnudez*, ed. G. Agamben, trans. Cristina Sardoy (Buenos Aires: Adriana Hidalgo Editora, 2011), 17–29.

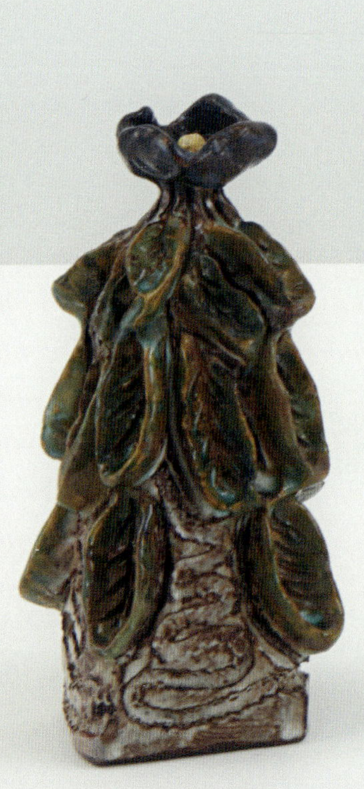
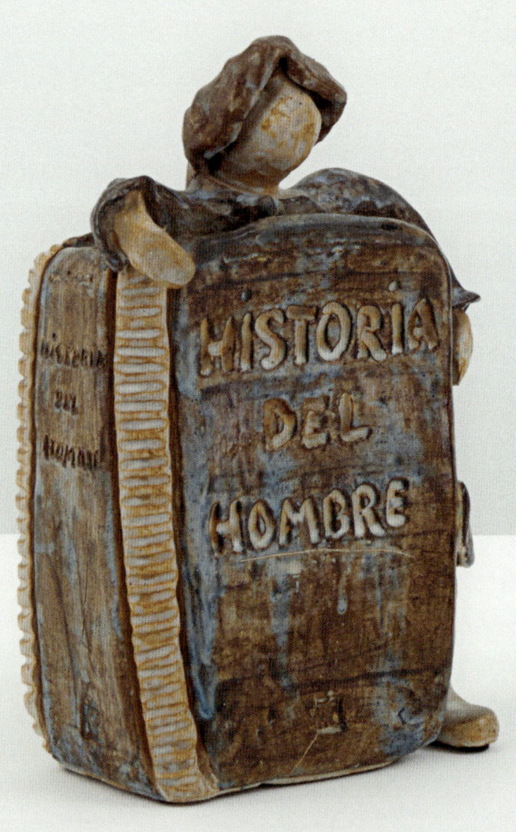

HISTORIA
DEL
HOMBRE

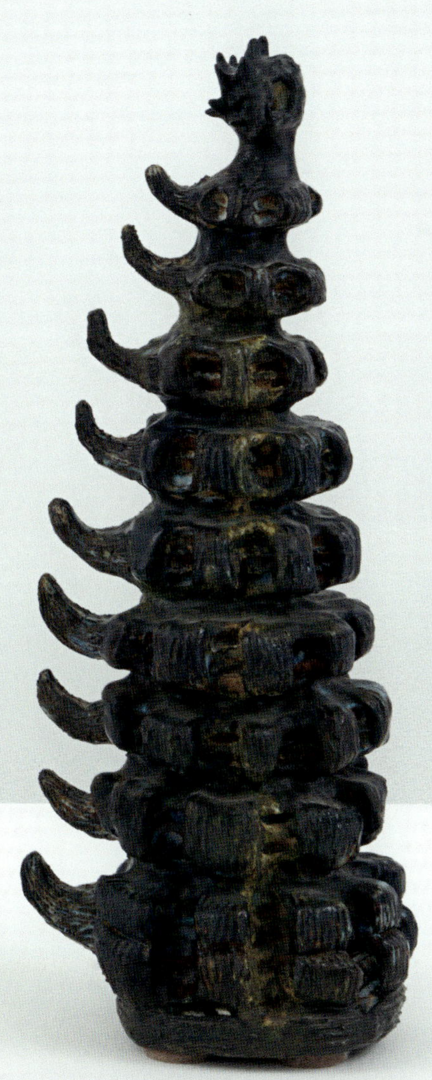

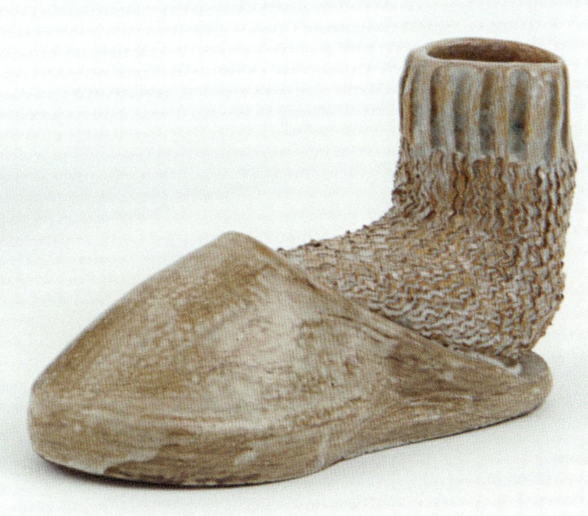

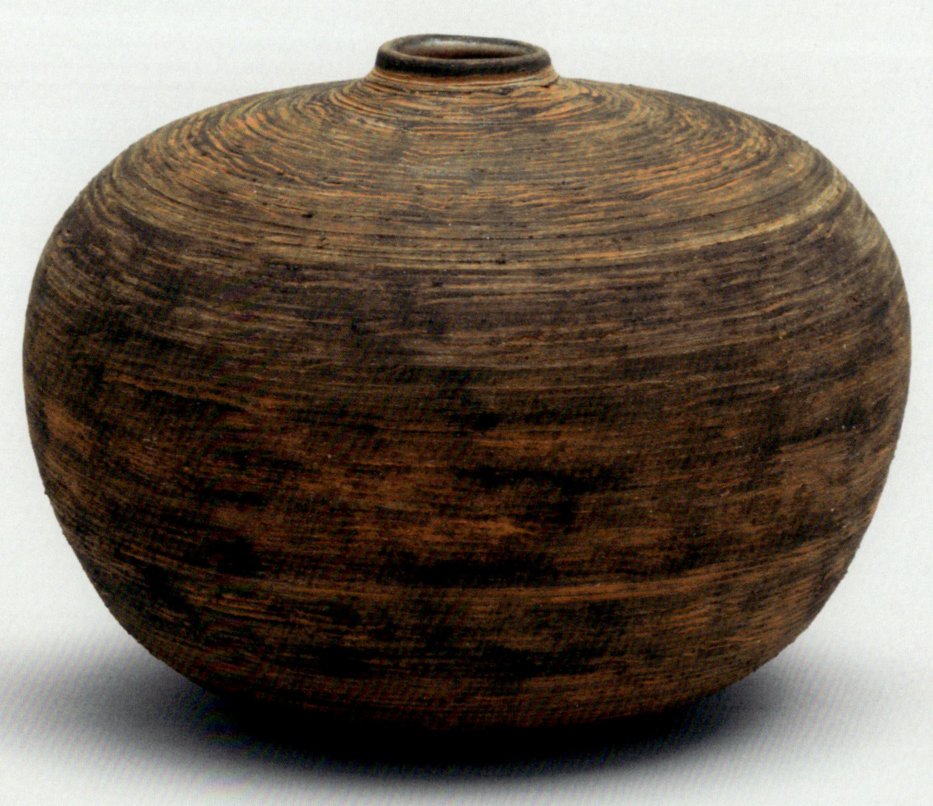

32   *Sin título* (Untitled), 1959

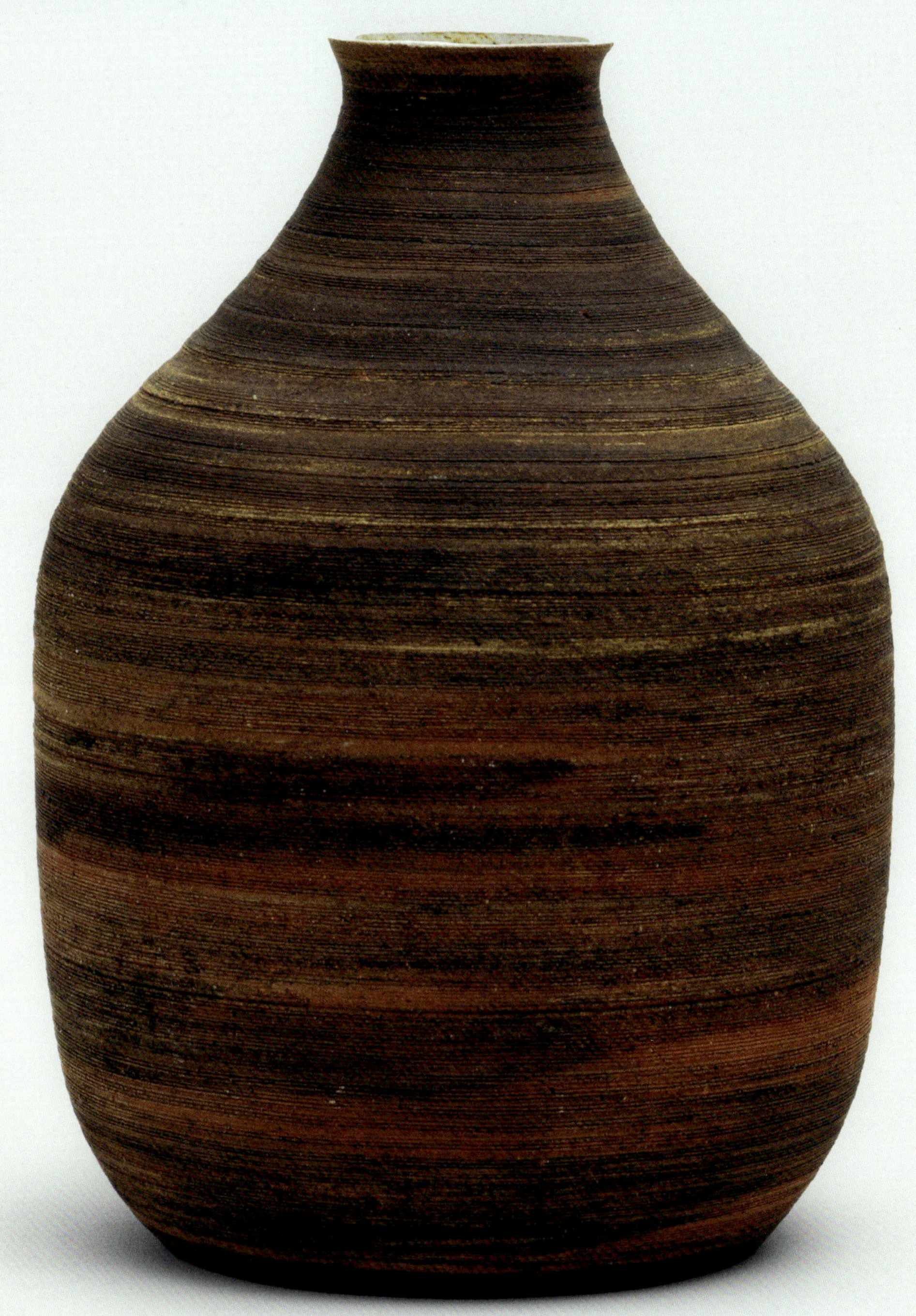

Sin título (Untitled), 1959   33

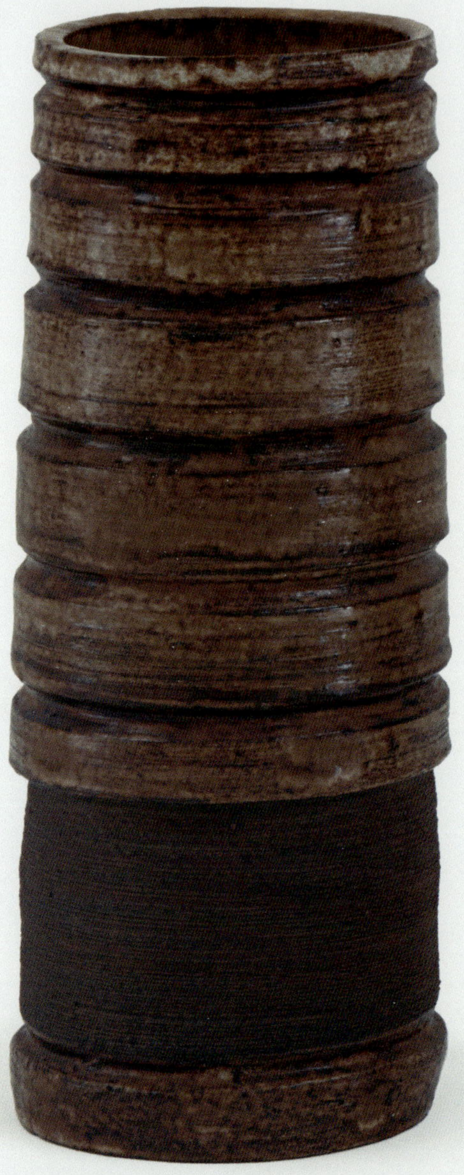
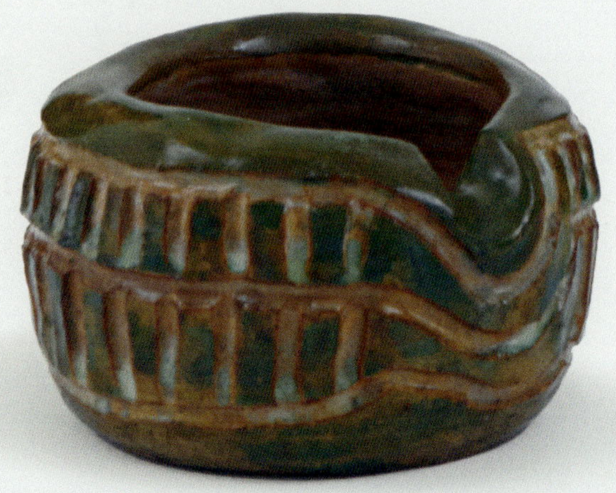

 Sin título (Untitled), 1961

Sin título (Untitled), 1965

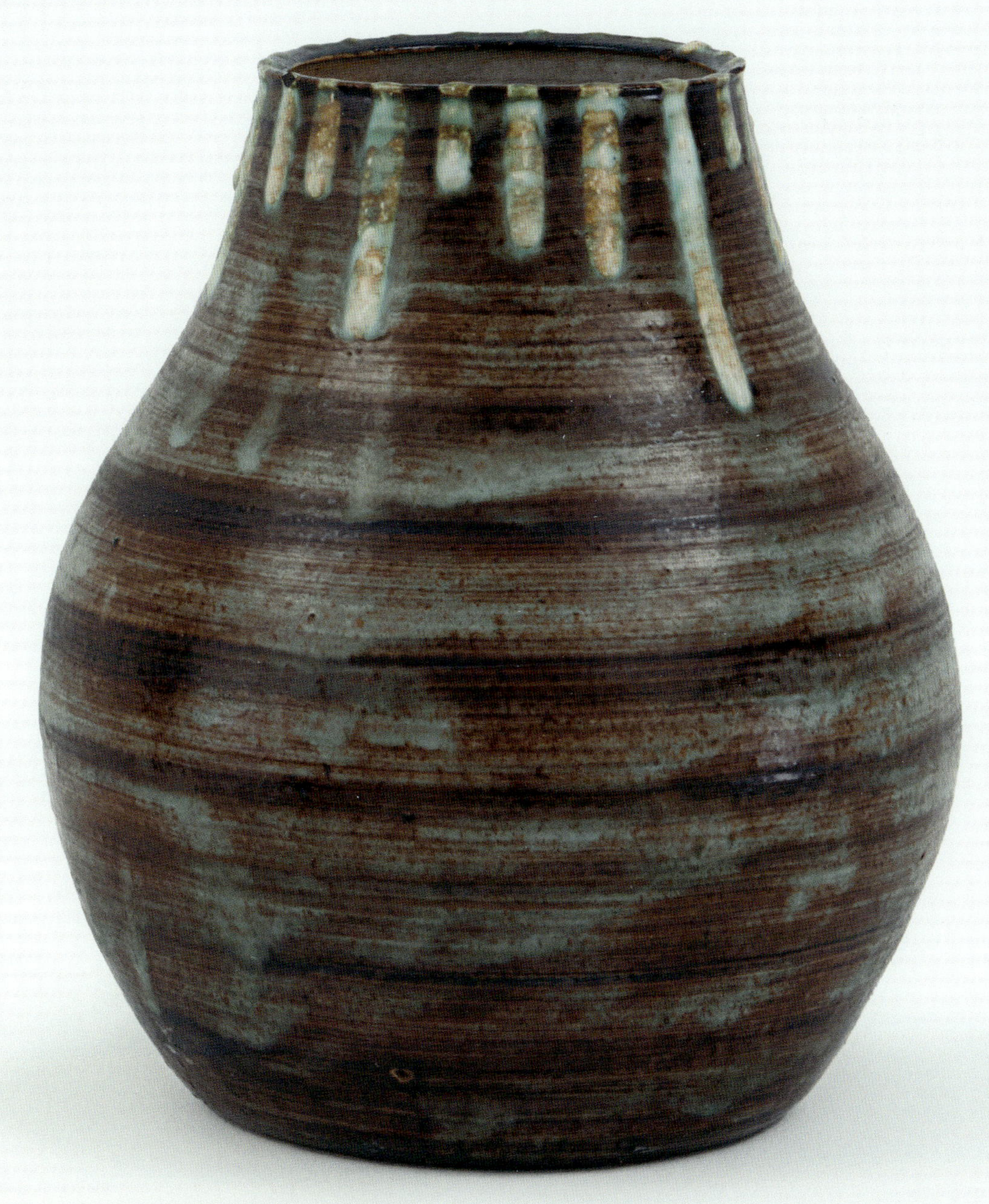

Sin título (Untitled), 1964   35

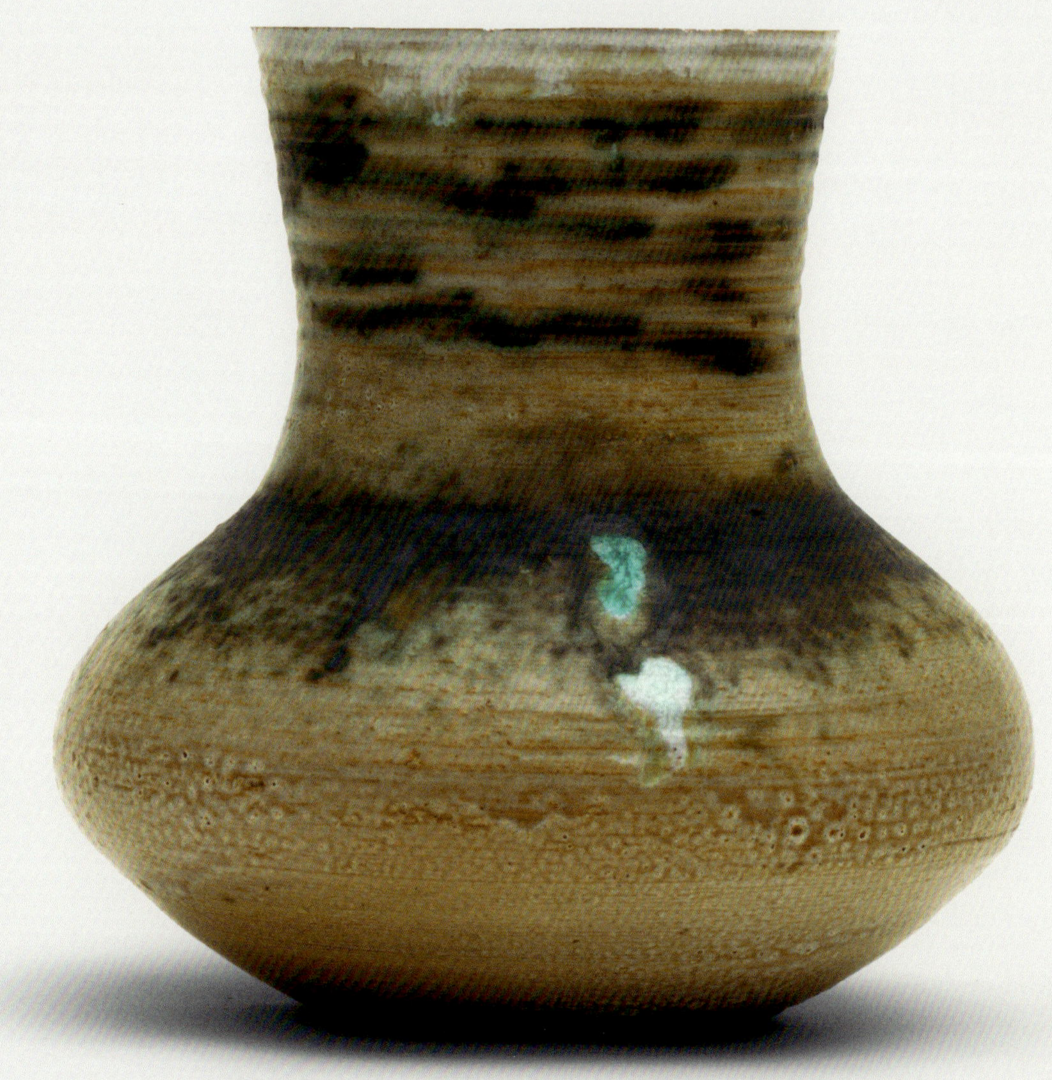

36   *Sin título* (Untitled), 1969

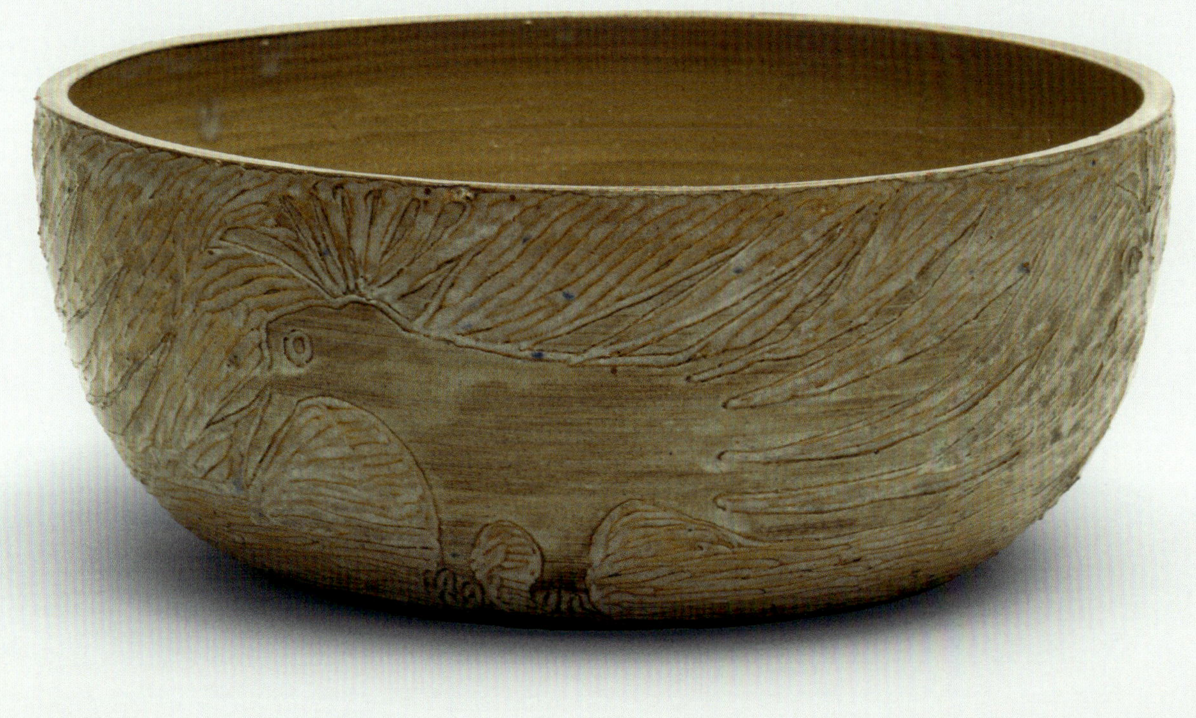

Sin título (Untitled), 1972   37

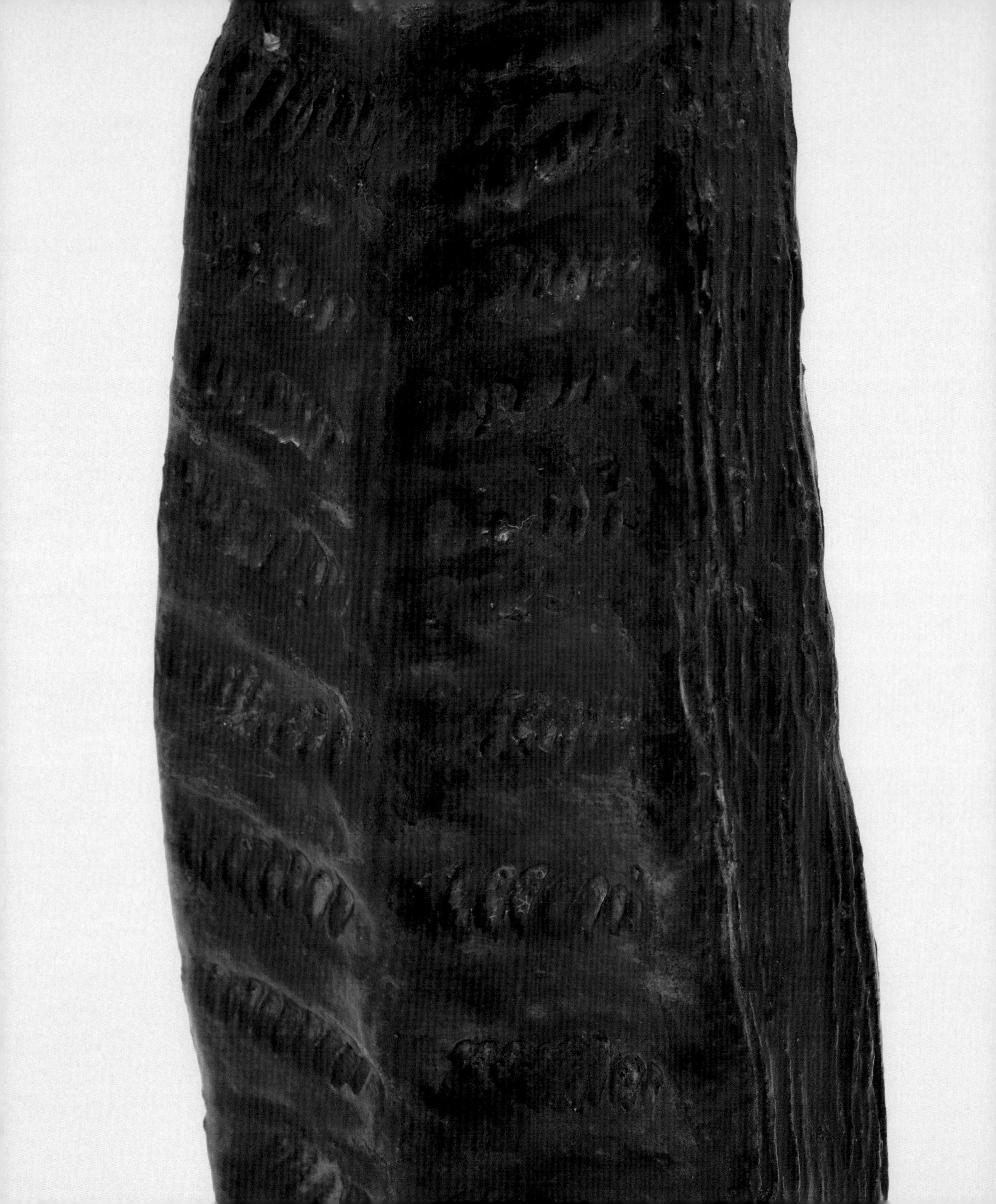

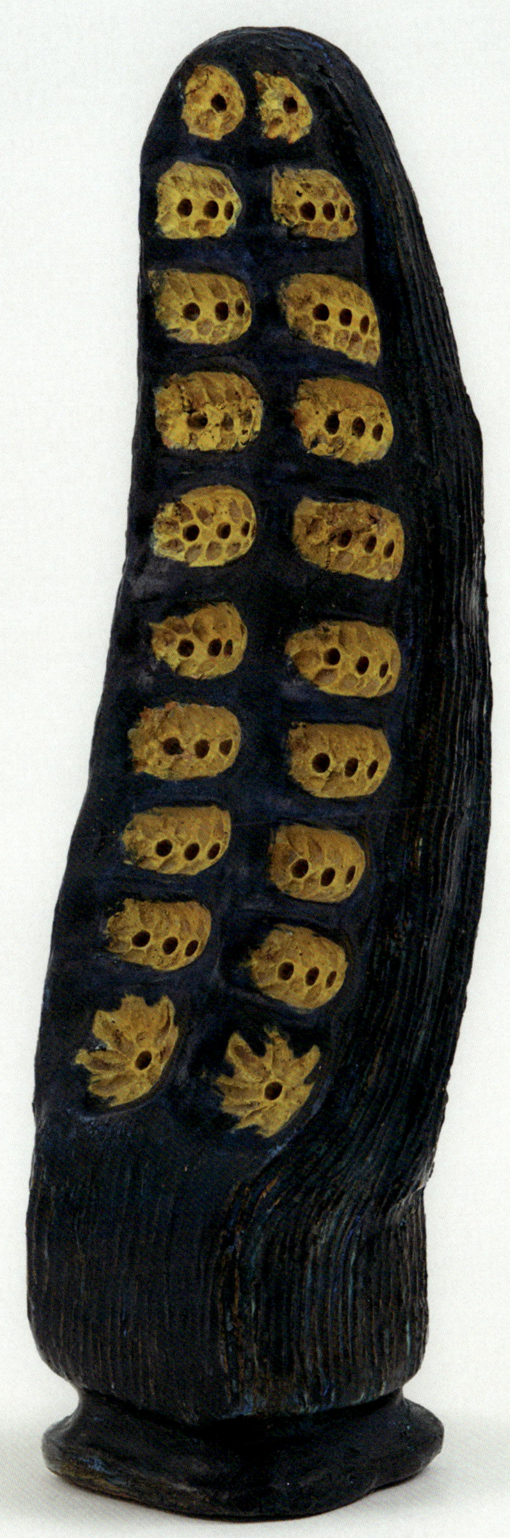

Lengua tótem (Totem Tongue), 1966   39

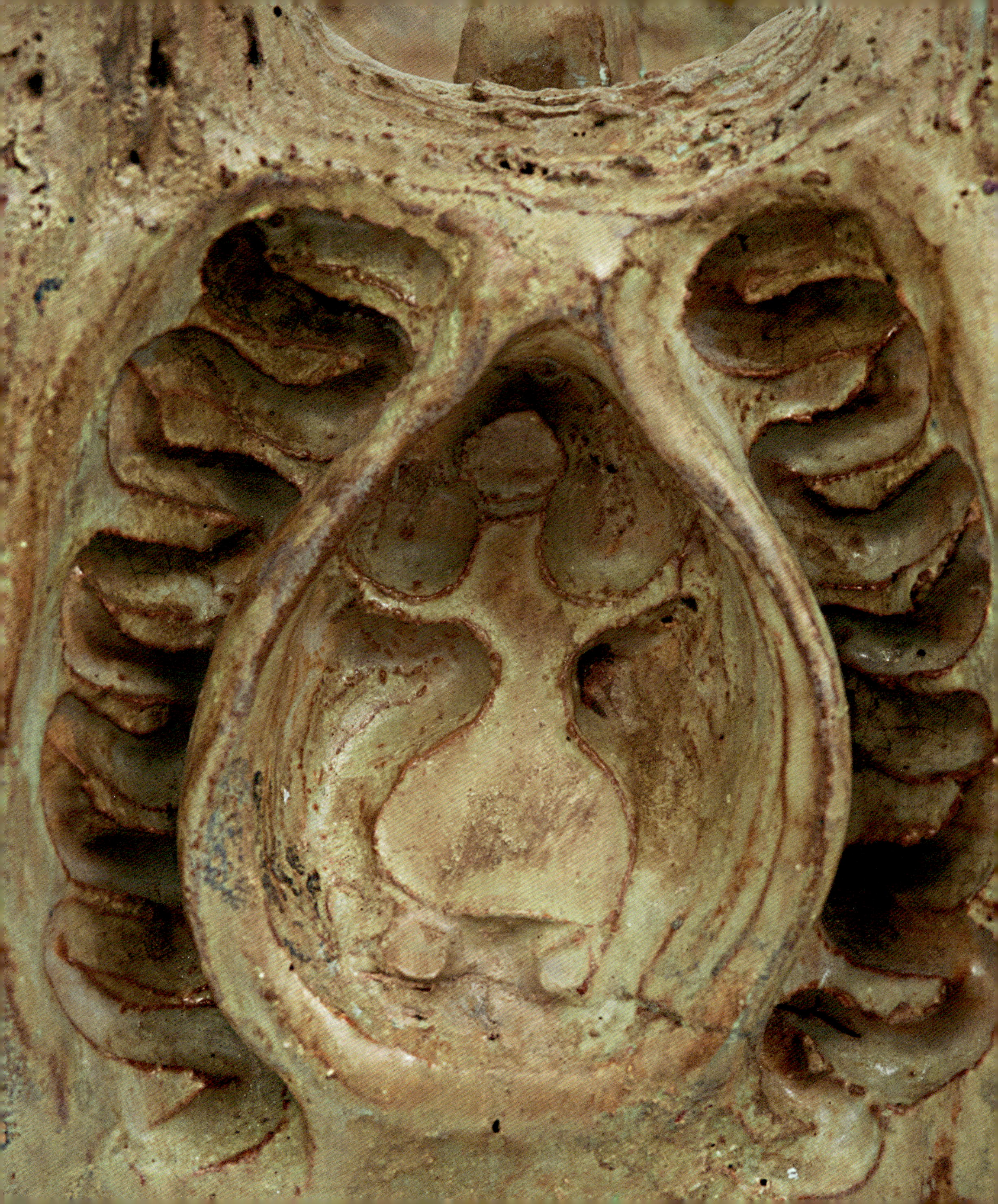

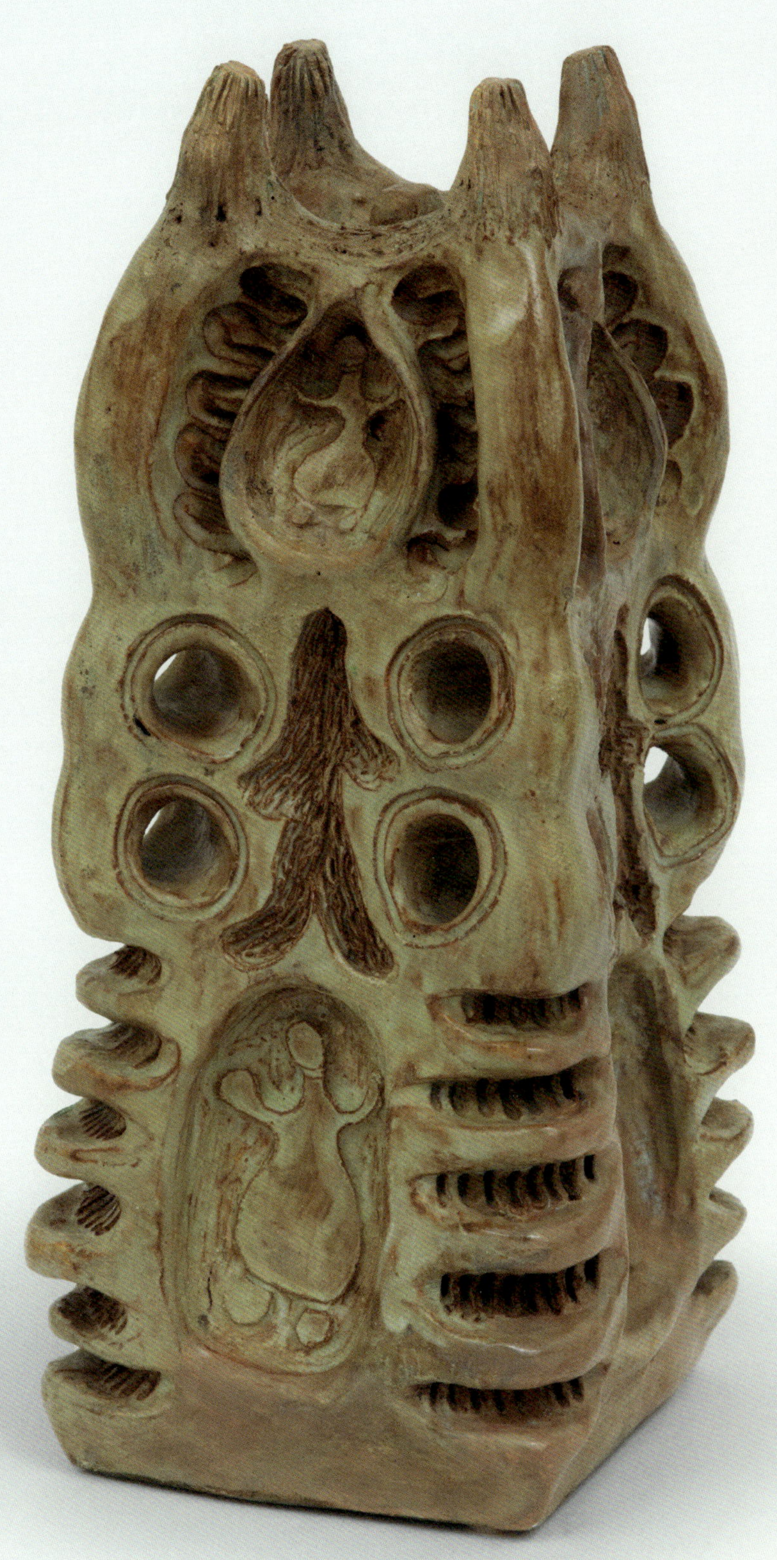

Sin título (Untitled), 1966   41

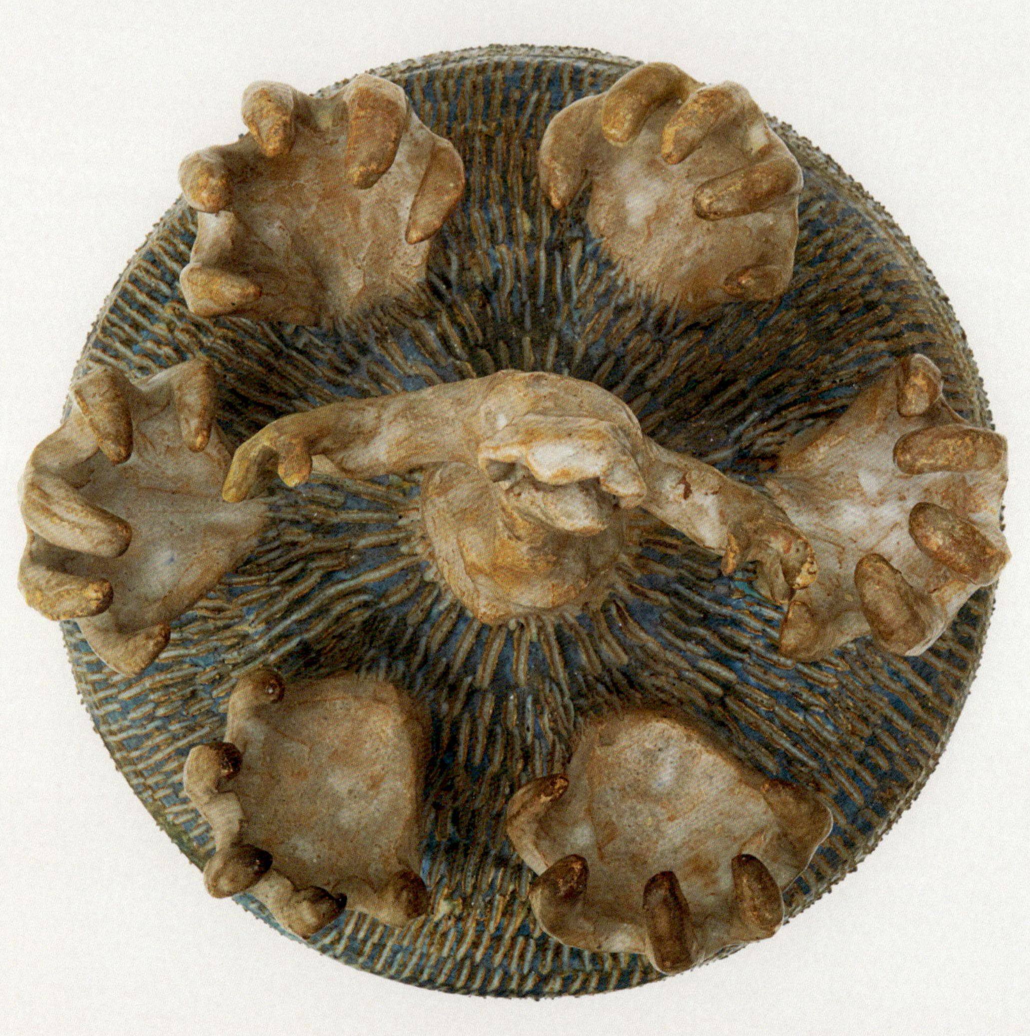

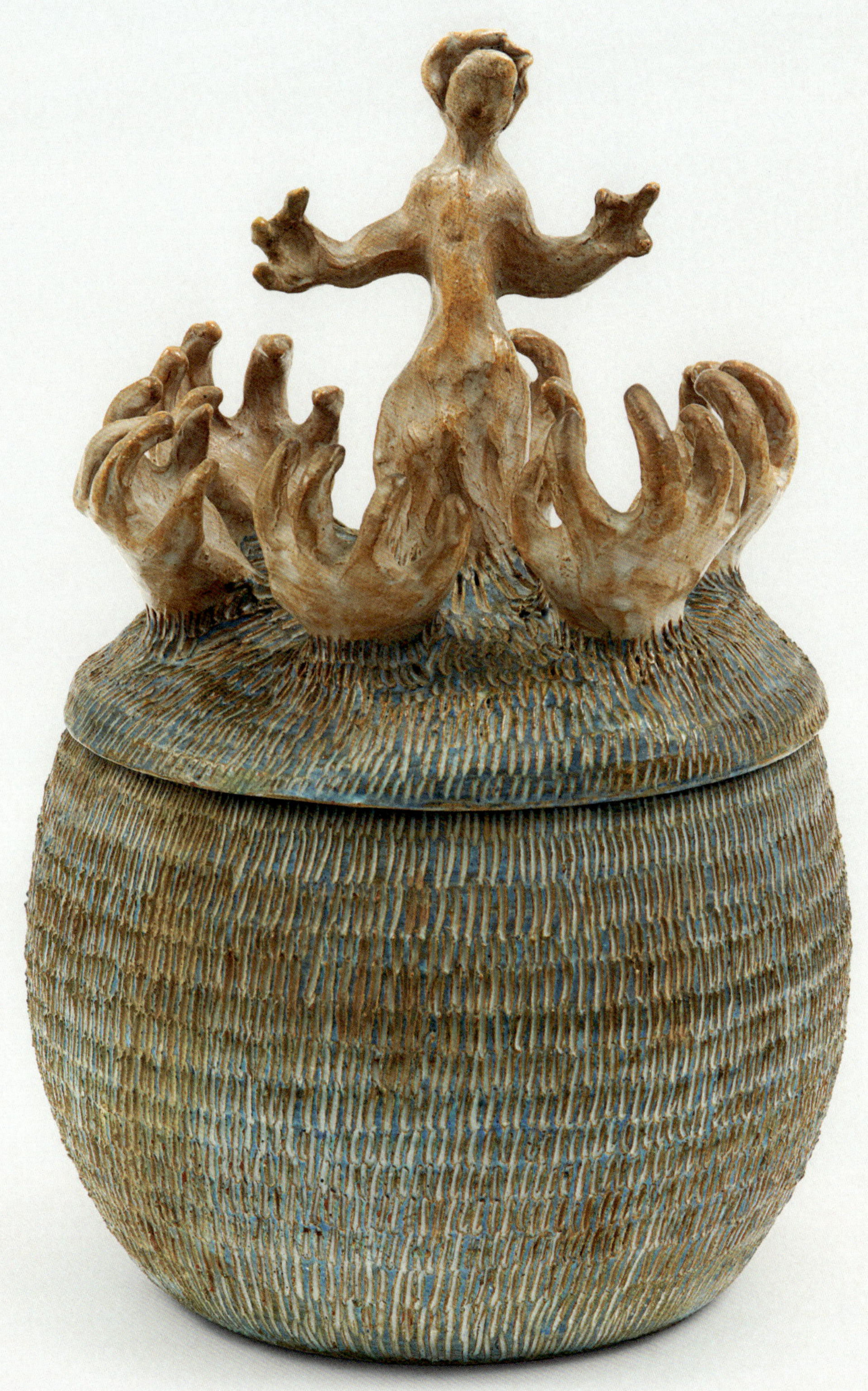

Vasija con personaje (Vessel with Personage), 1969   43

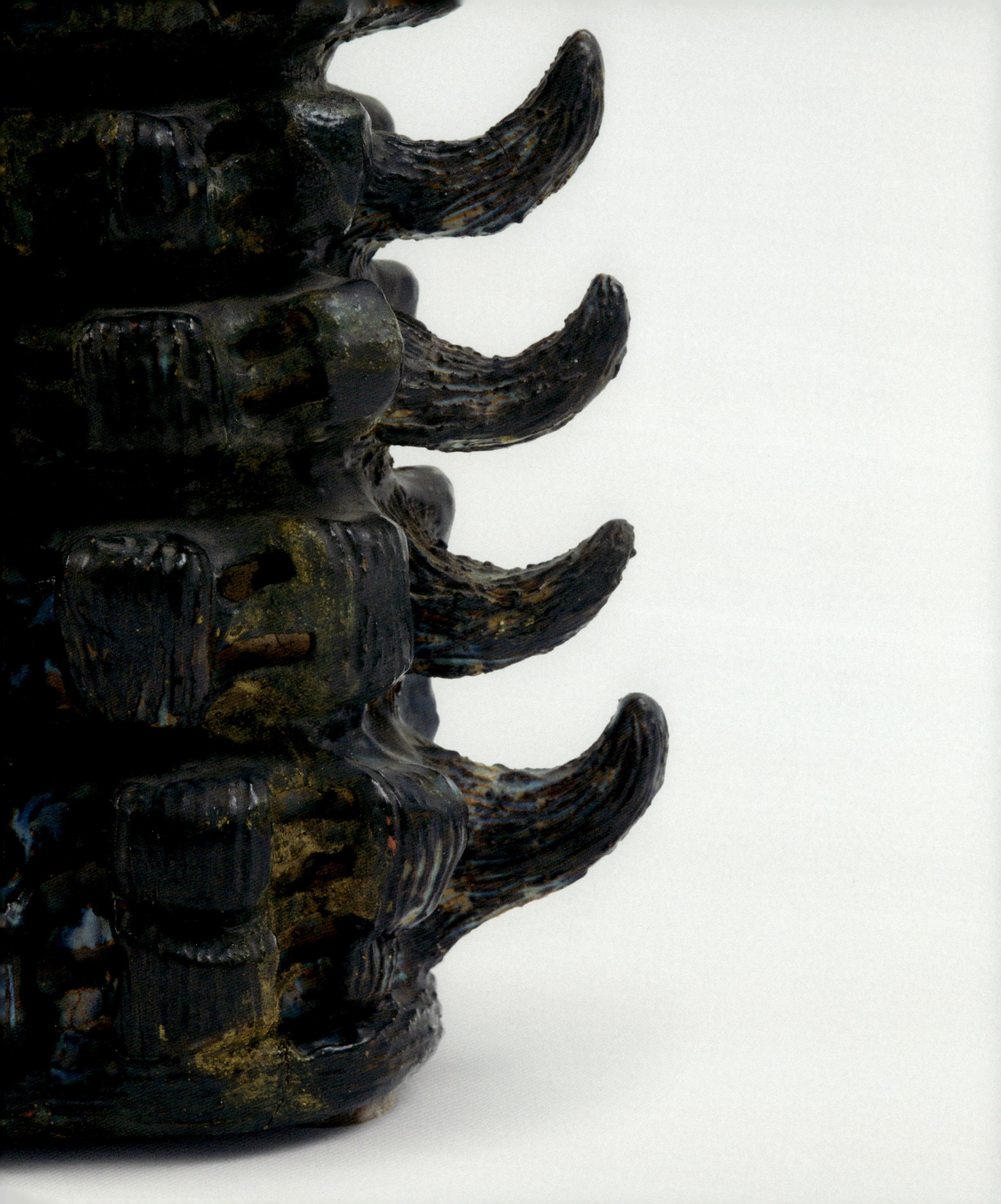

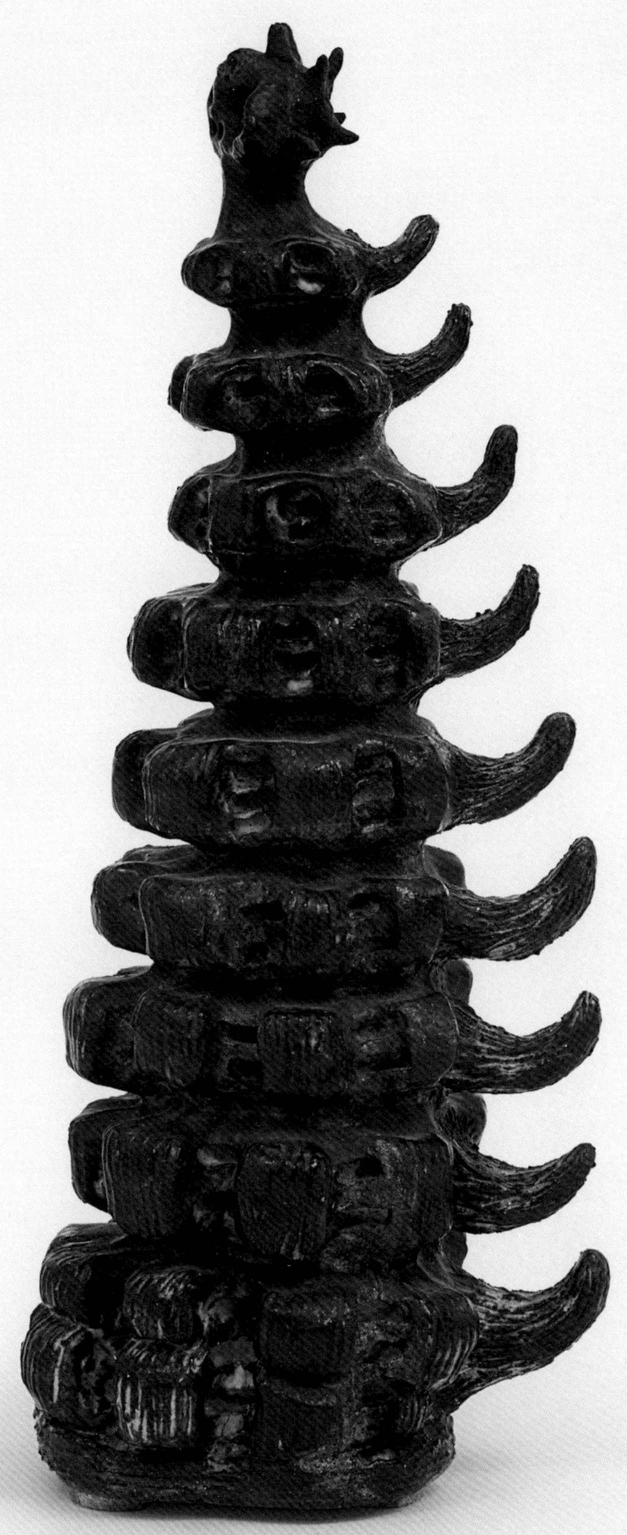

Hábitat dragón (Habitat Dragon), 1967   45

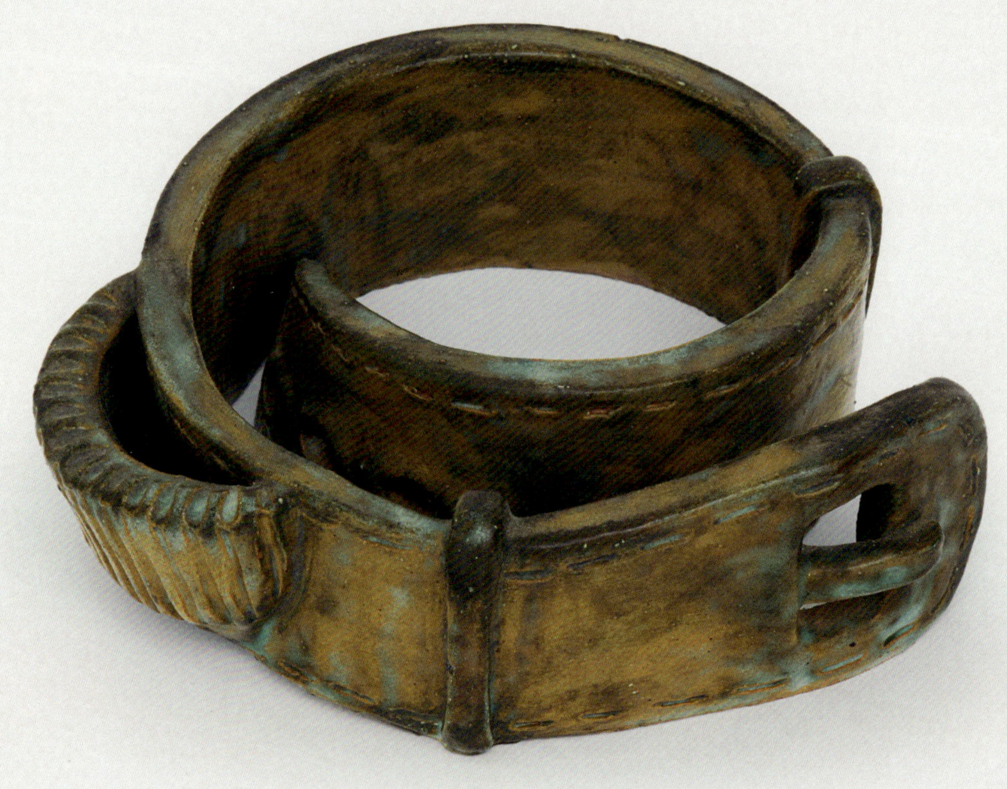

46   *Cinturón con cartera* (Belt with Purse), 1971

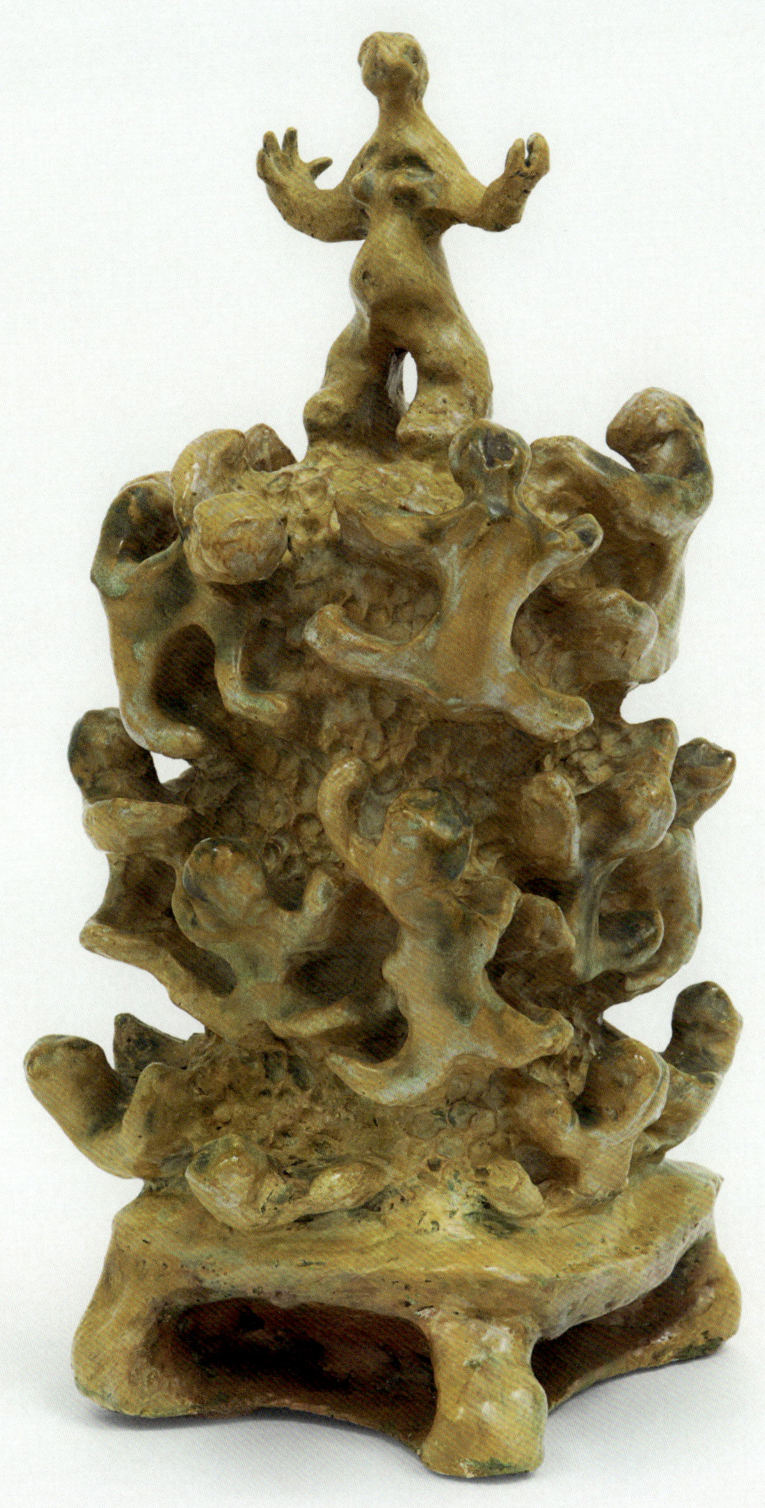

Bastión (Bastion), 1967 47

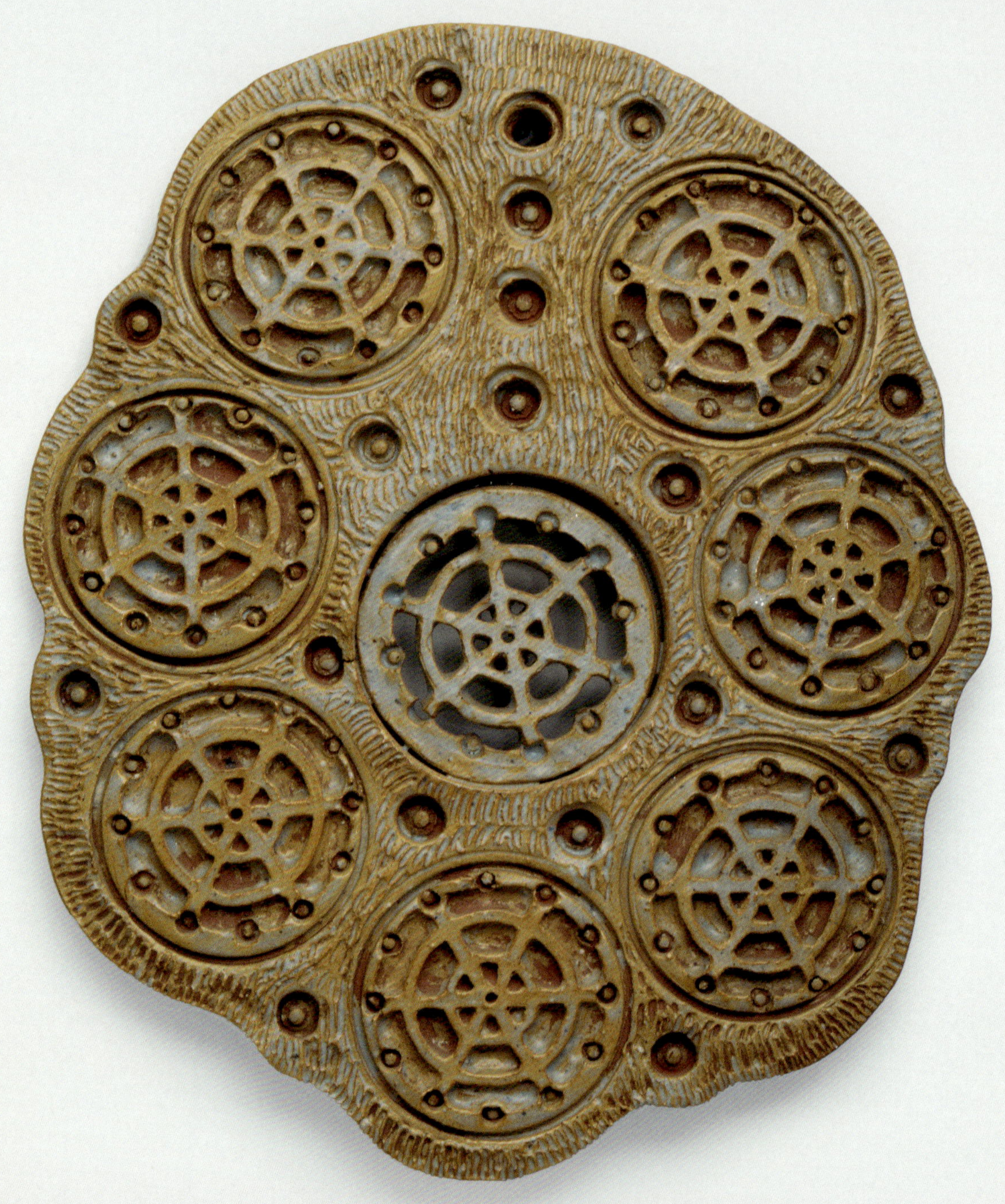

48   *Monumento a la rueda* (Wheel Monument), 1969

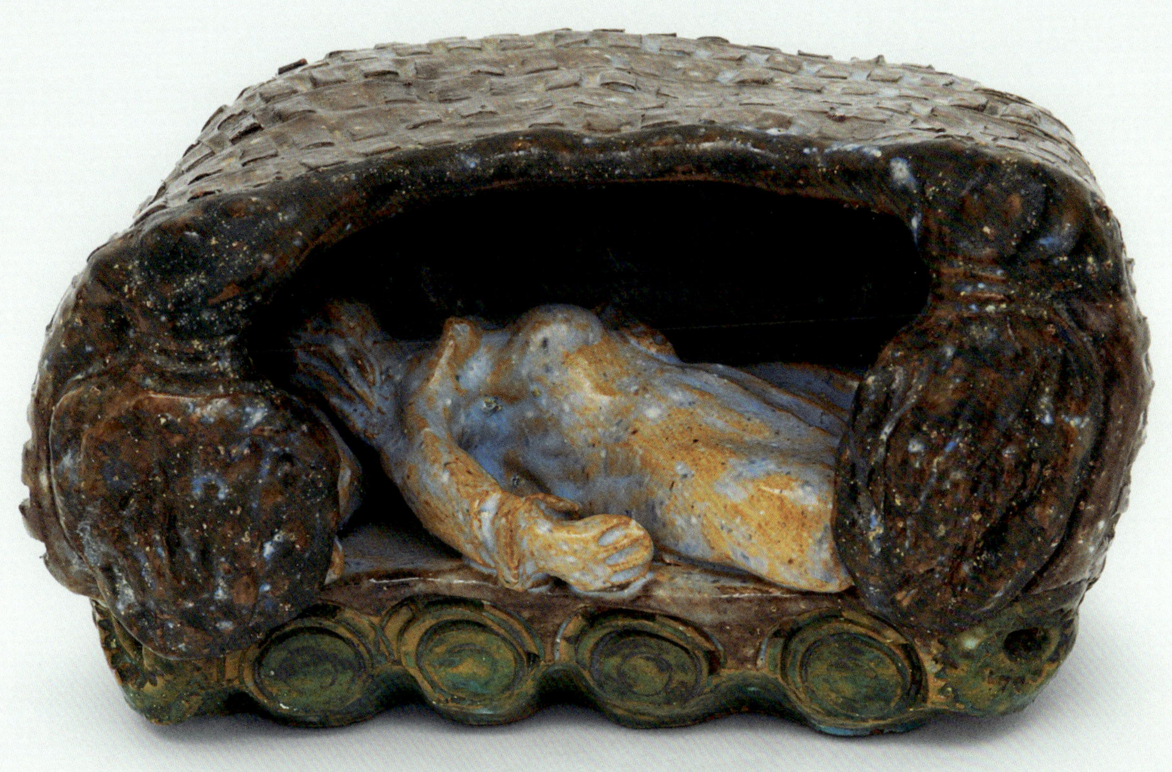

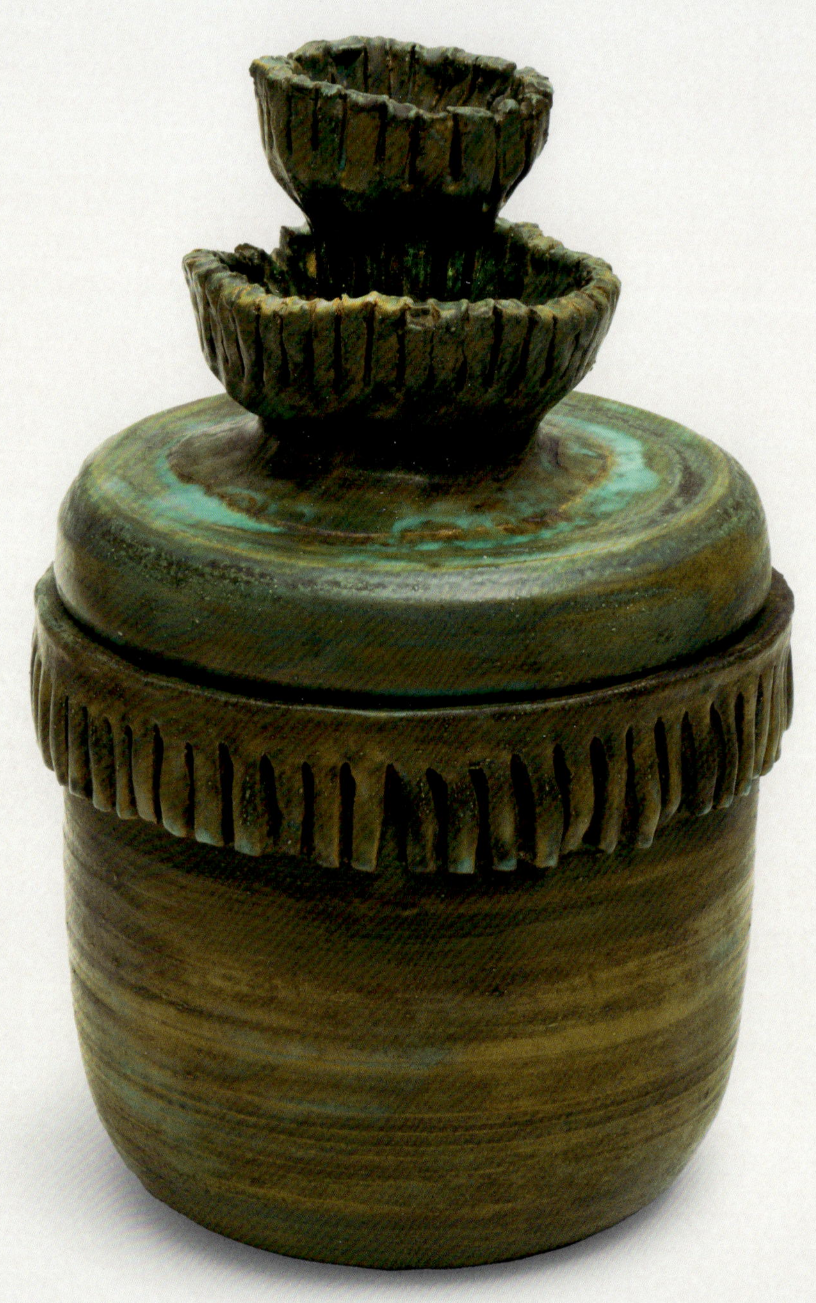

50   *Sin título* (Untitled), 1972

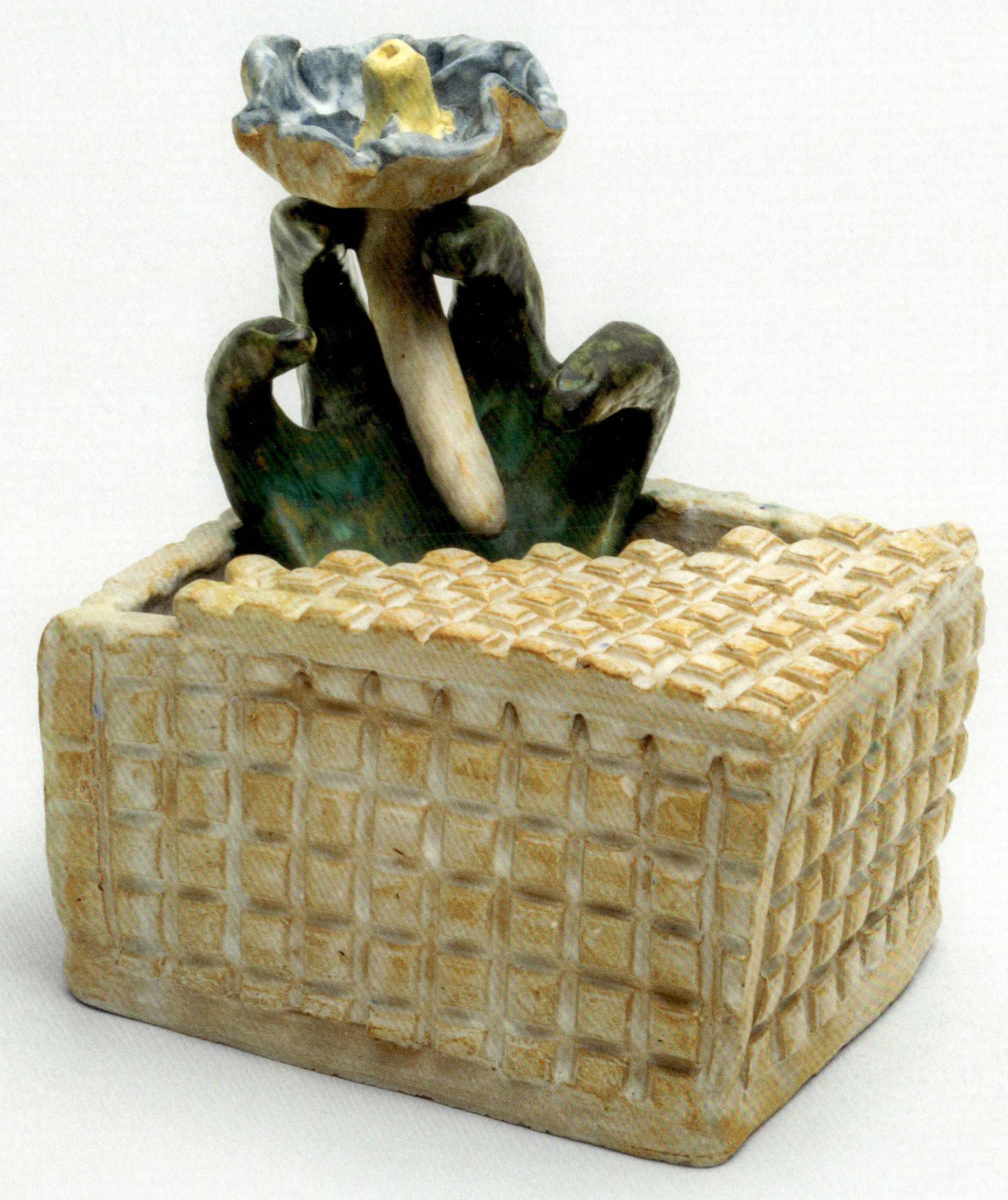

Sin título (Untitled), 1970   51

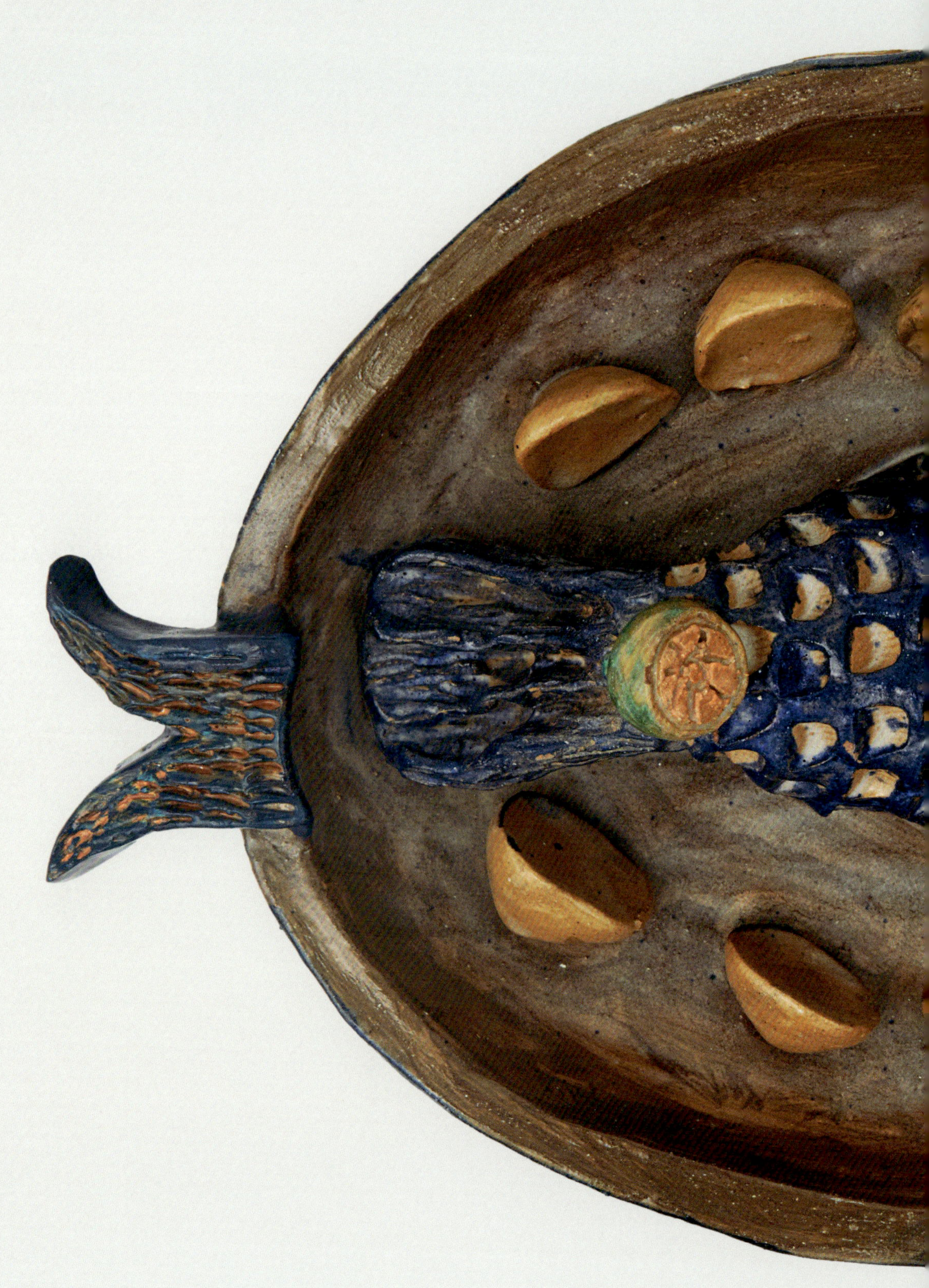

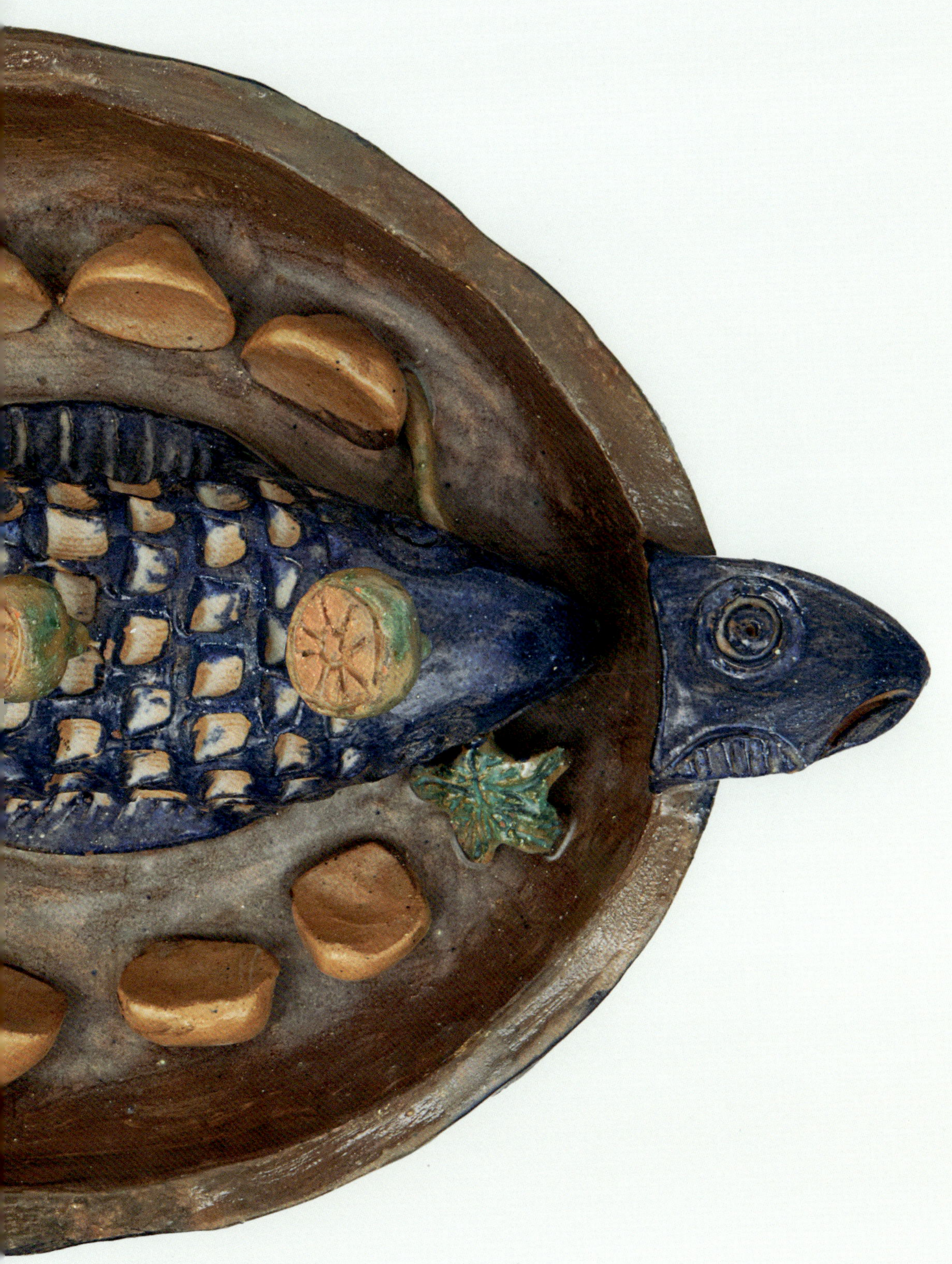

Bacalao al limón (Cod with Lemon), 1973   53

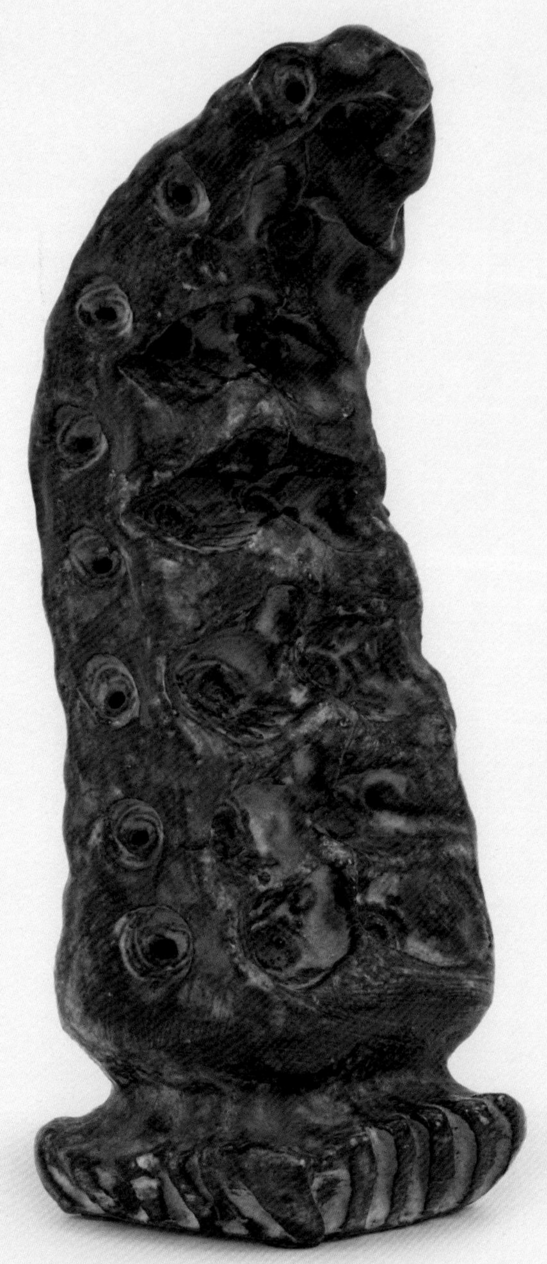

54   *Lengua* (Tongue), 1966

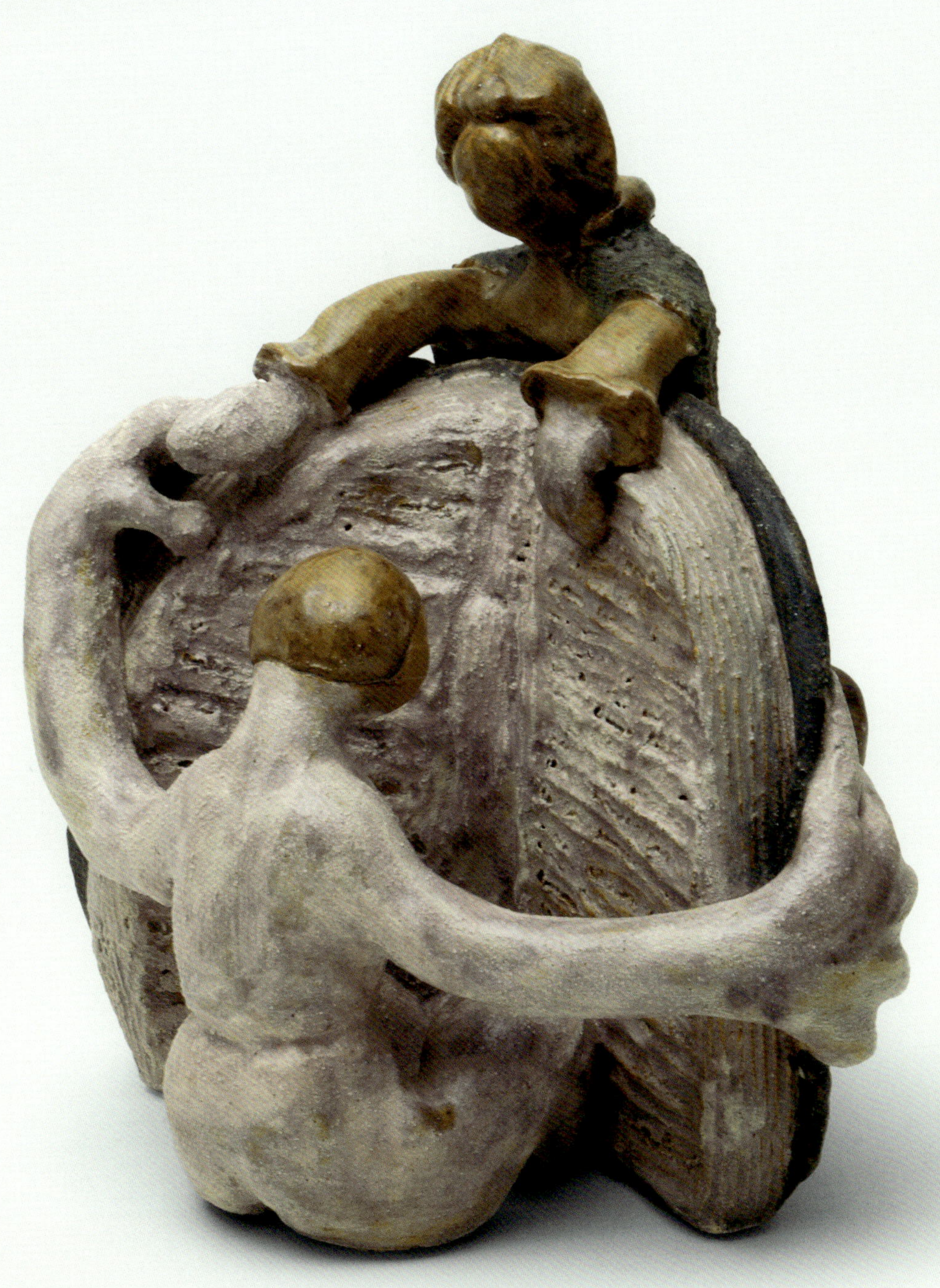

Comunicación (Communication), 1975   55

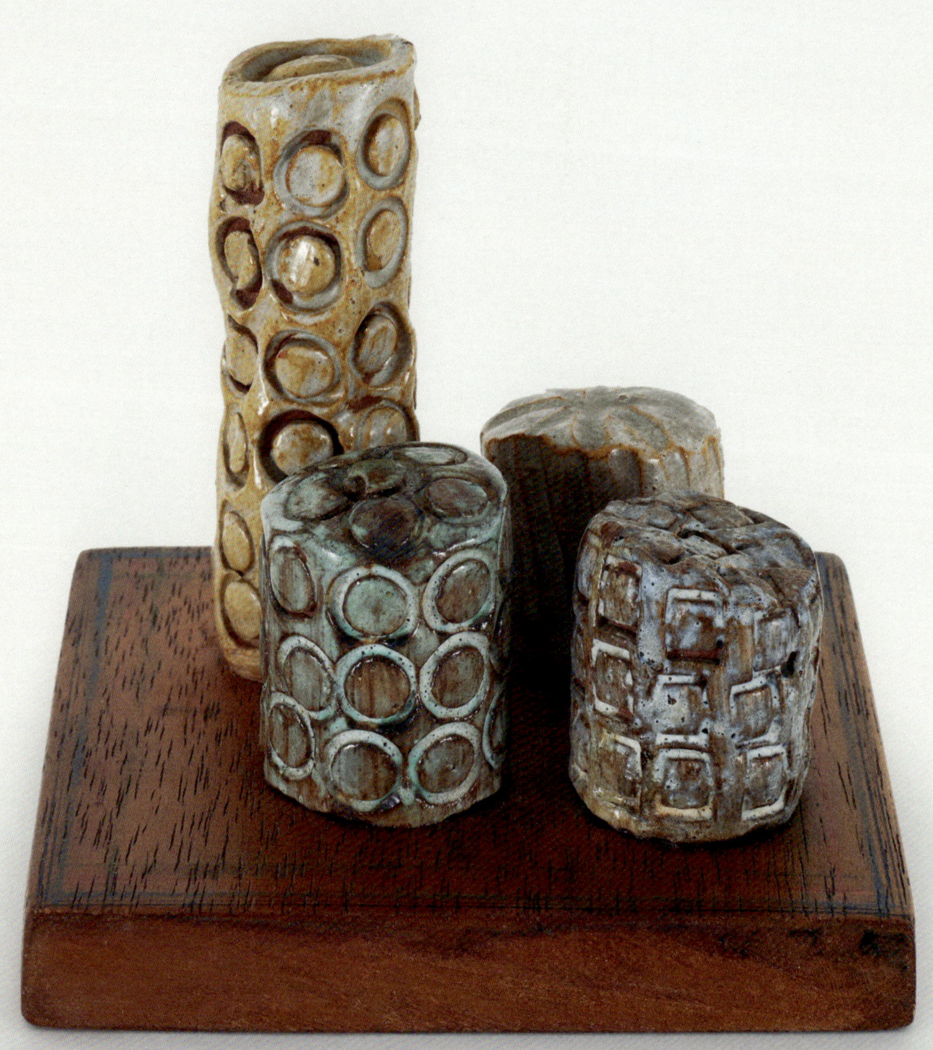

56   *Sin título* (Untitled), 1973

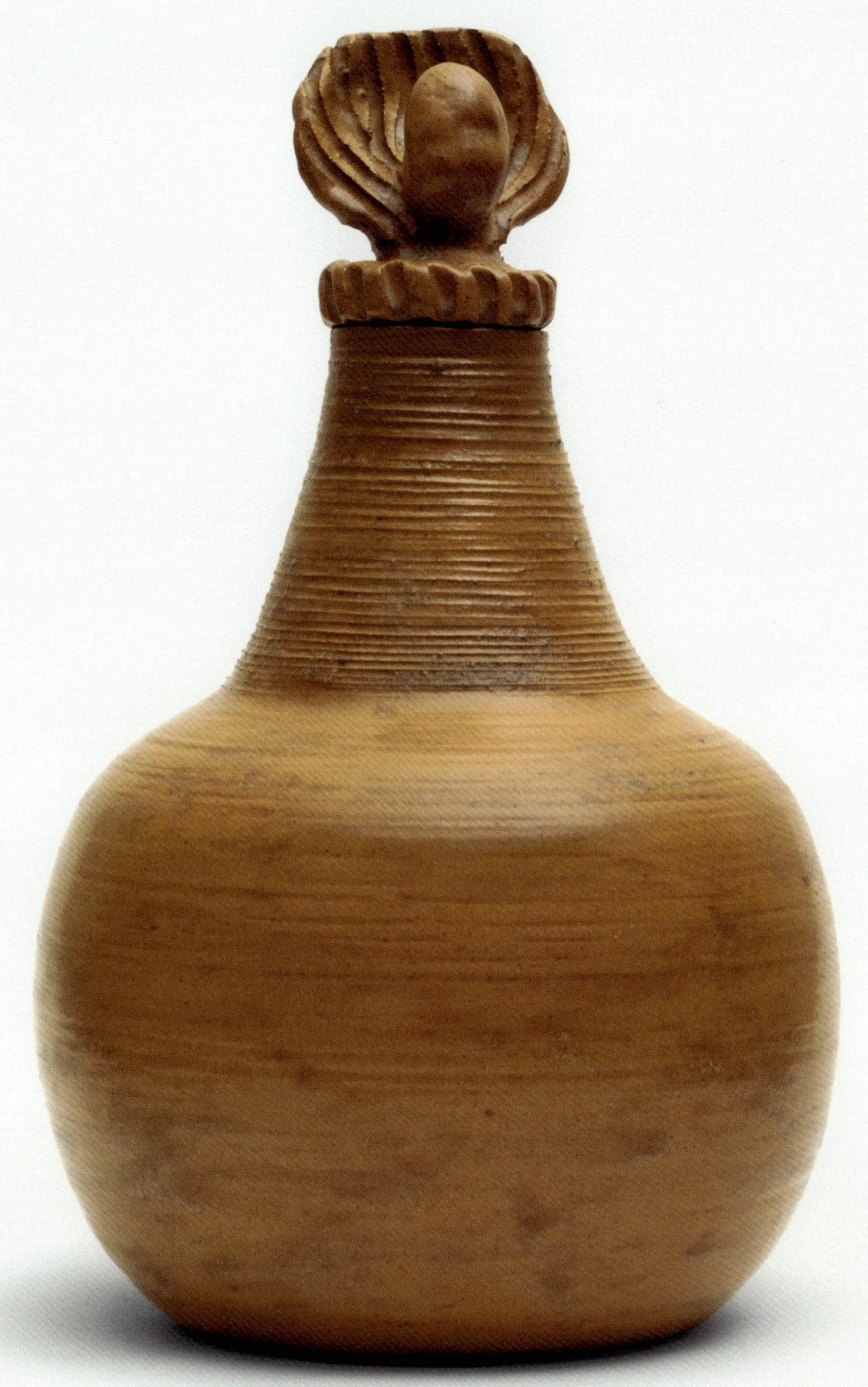

Sin título (Untitled), 1972   57

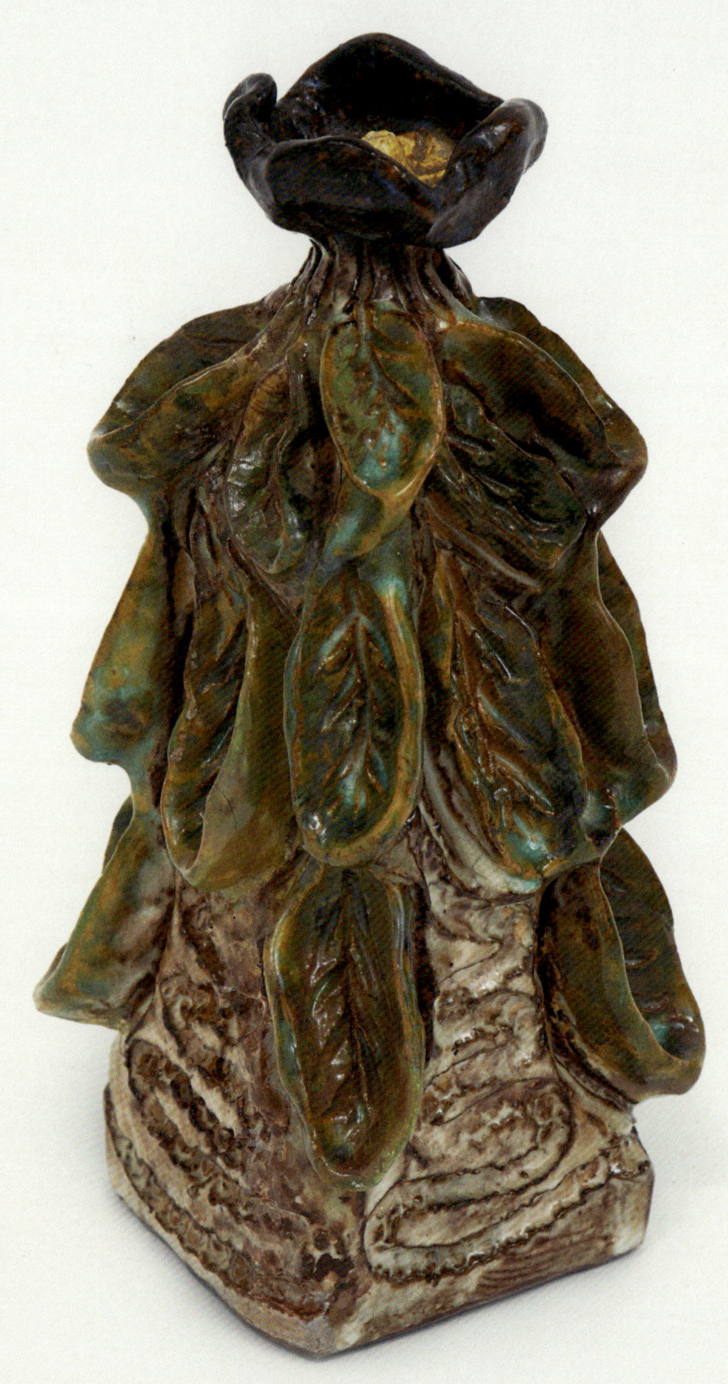

58 *Sin título* (Untitled), 1967

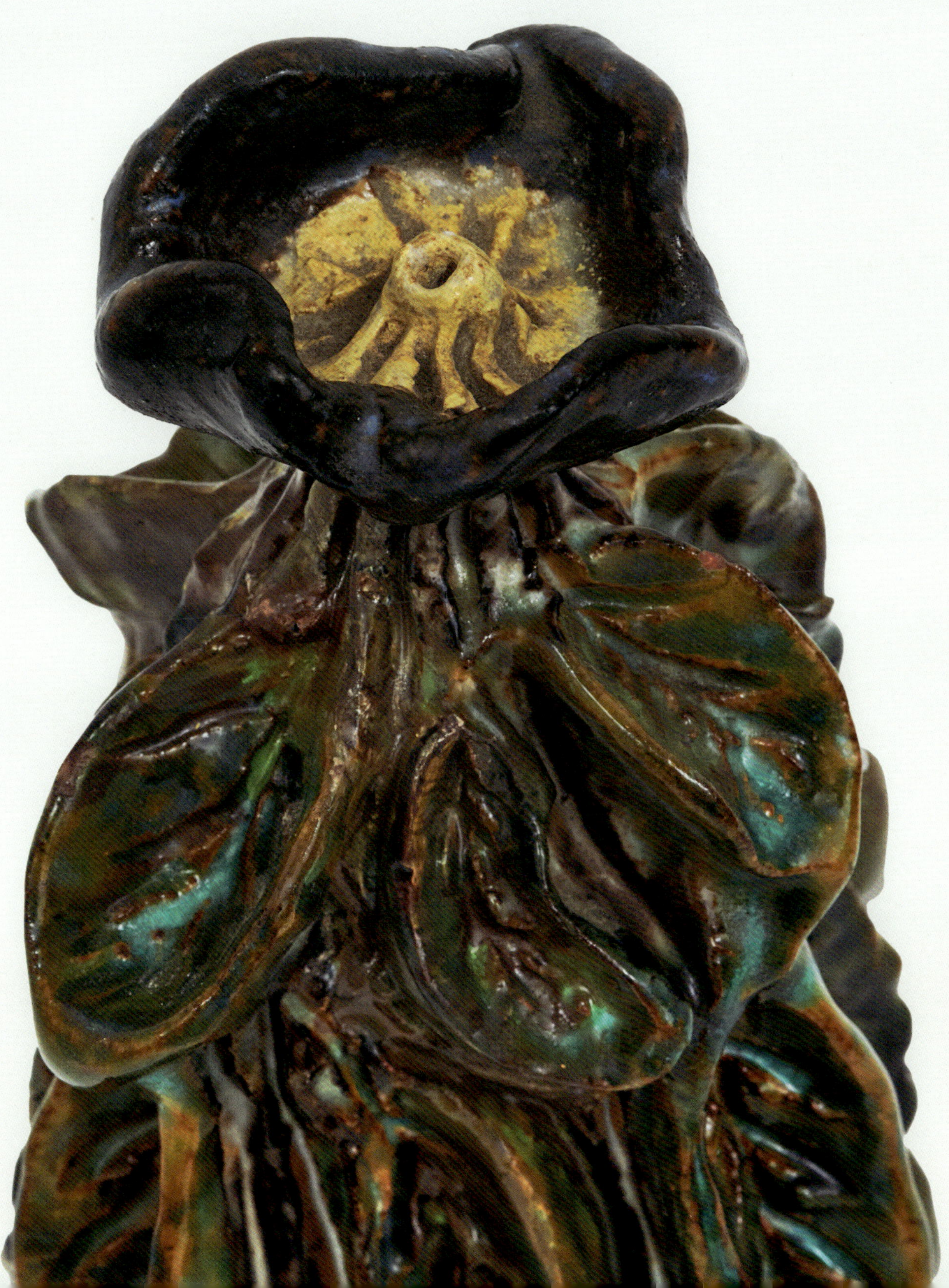

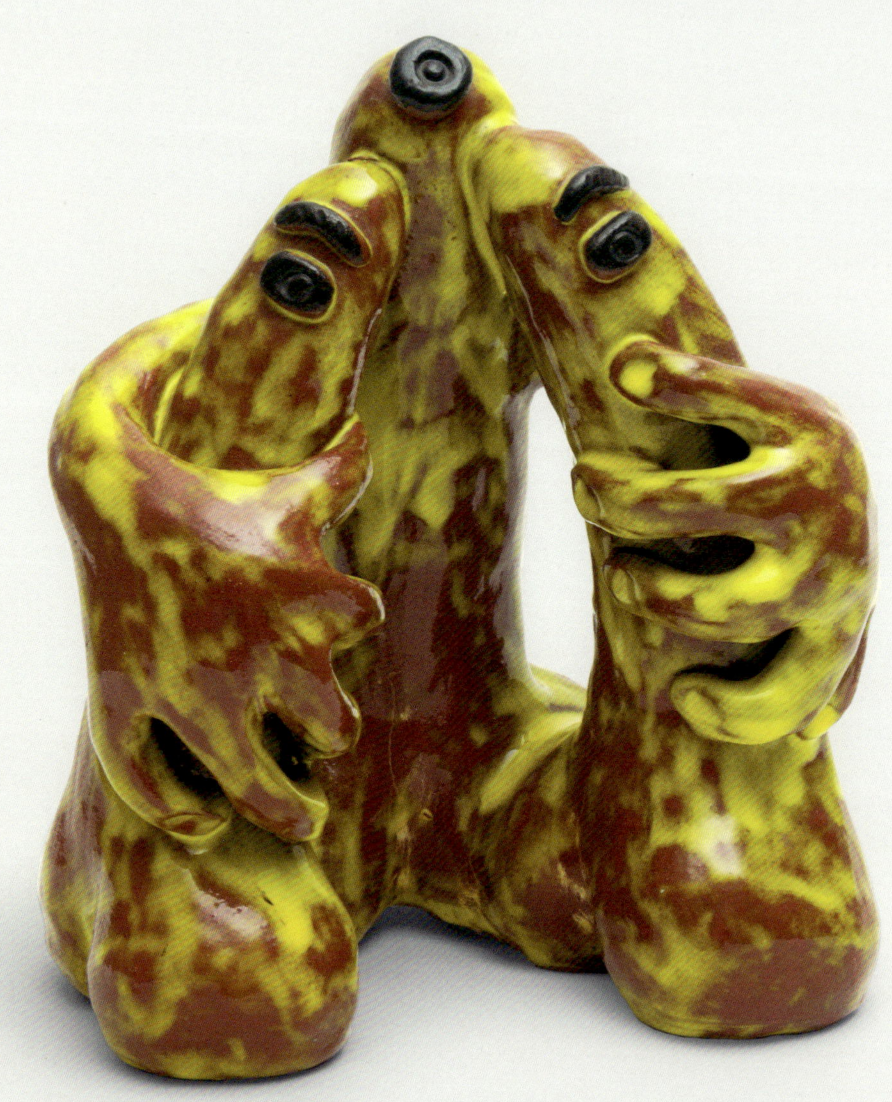

60   *Solidaridad* (Solidarity), 1973

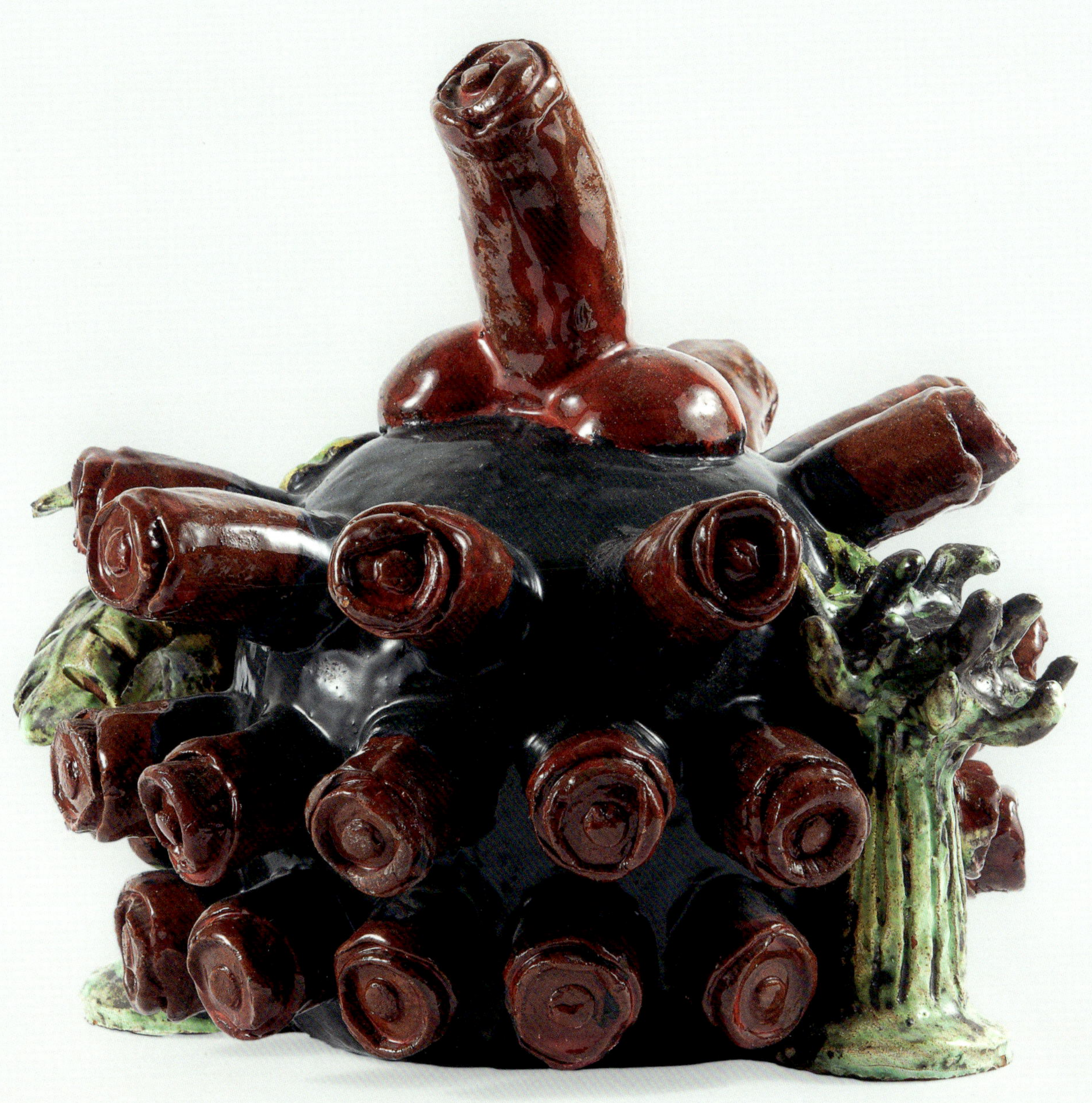

Y poblaron al mundo (And They Populated the World), 1973   61

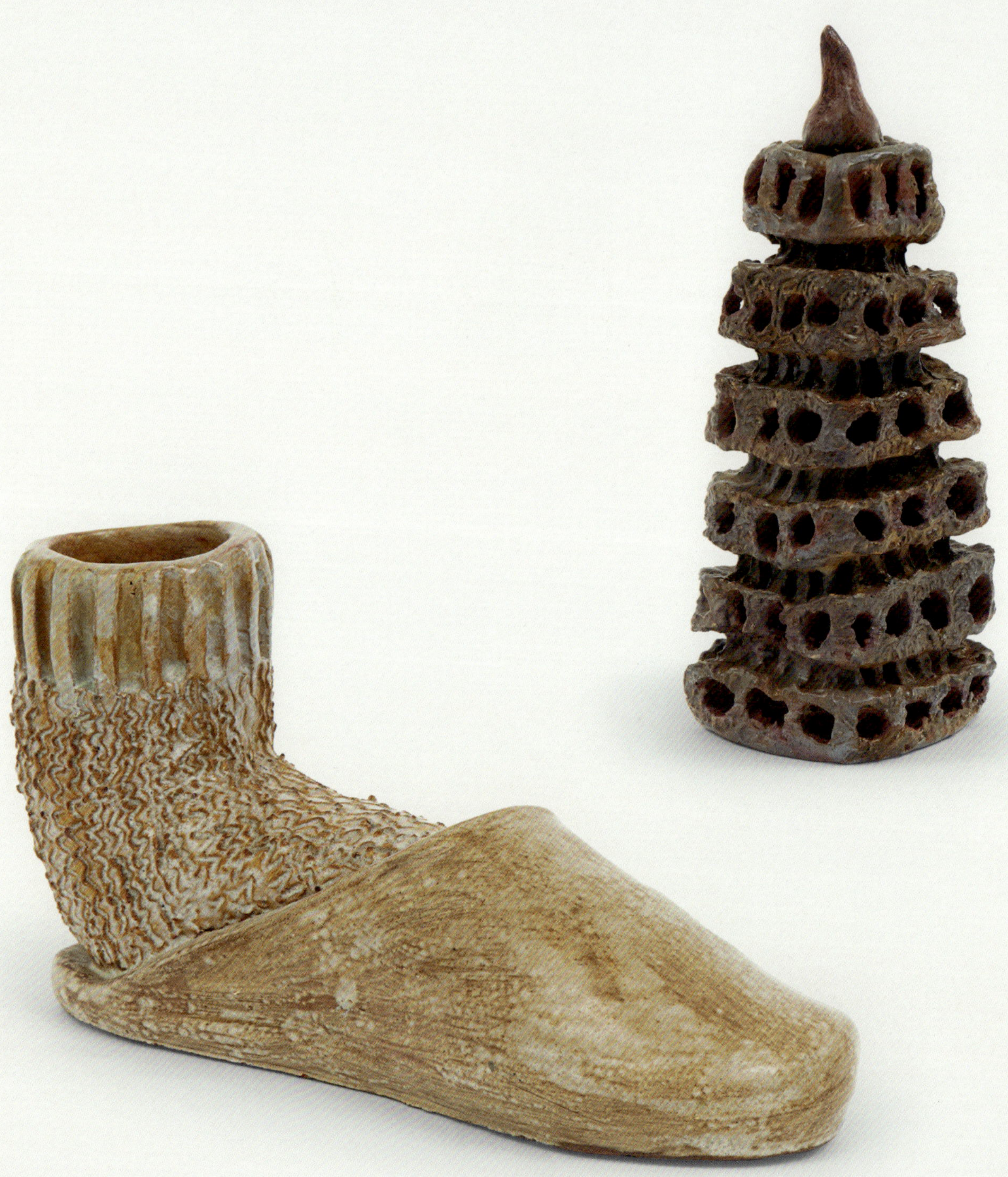

 Cuando me levanto (When I Wake Up), 1971   *Sin título* (Untitled), 1971

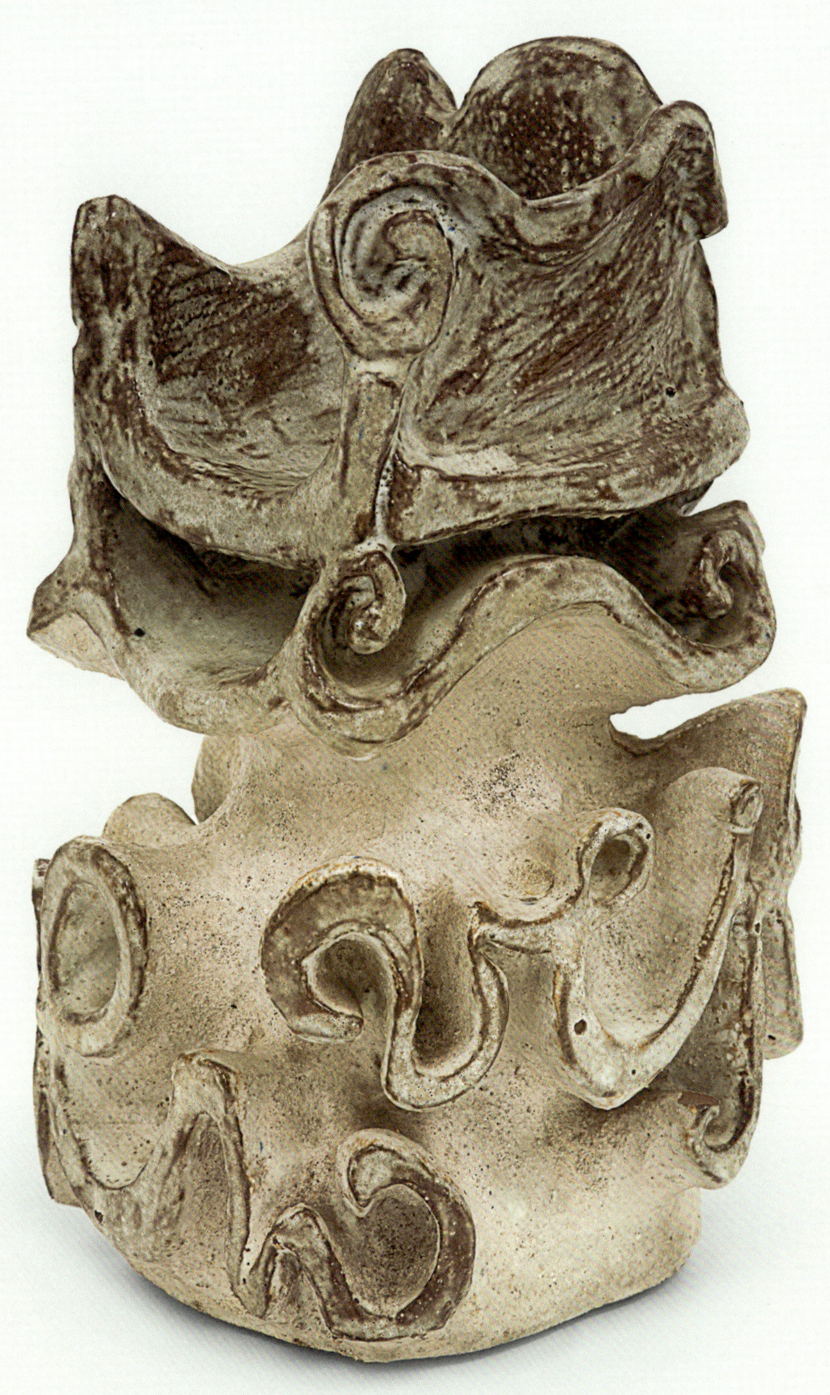

Vejez (Old Age), 1974   63

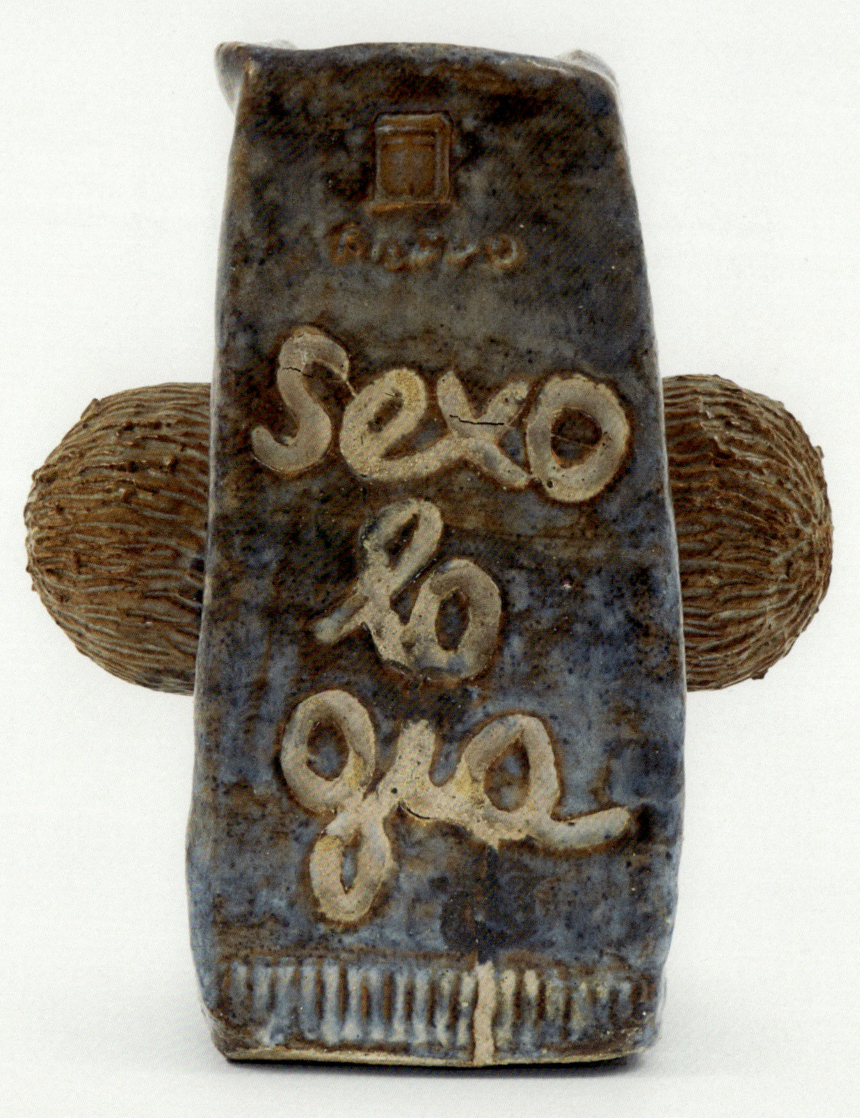

sexo
lo
gia

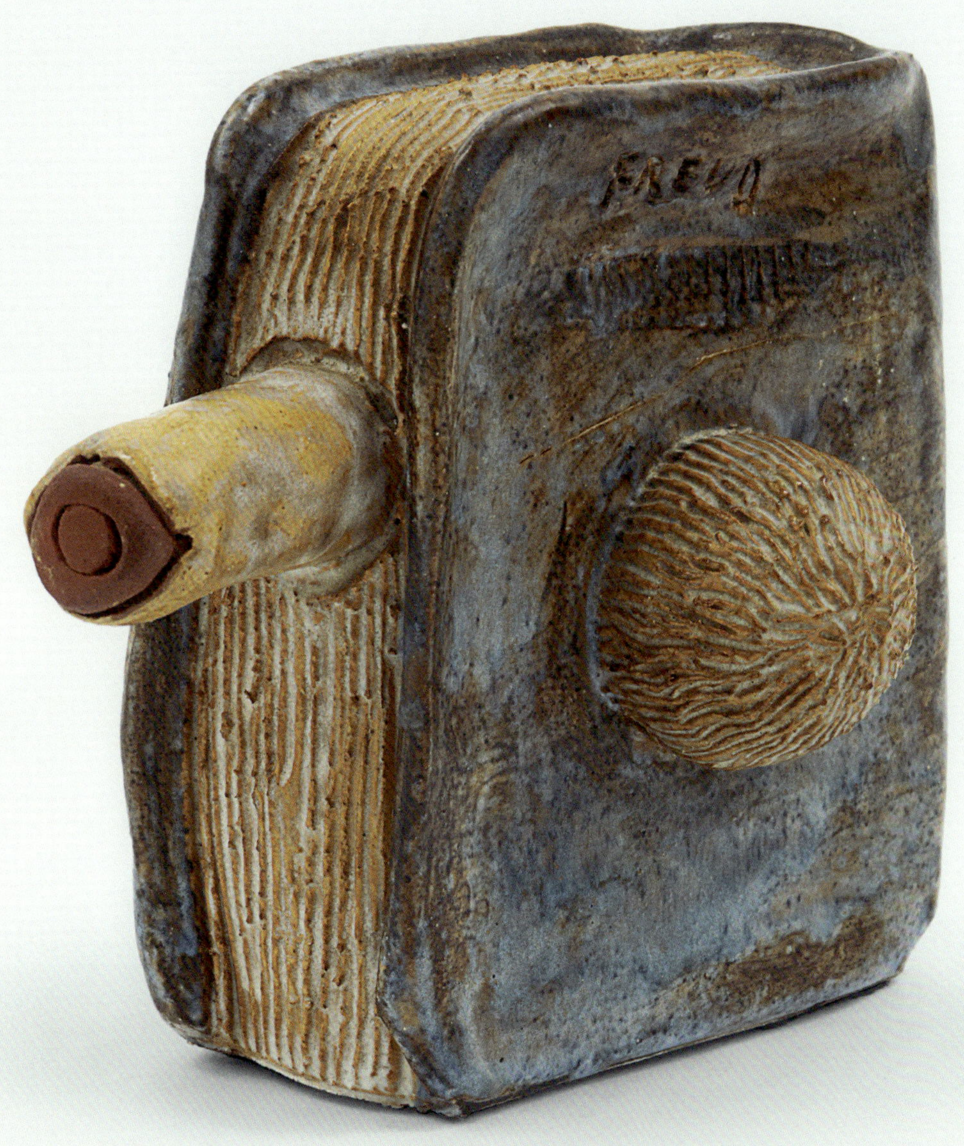

Freud, sexología (Freud, Sexology), 1975   65

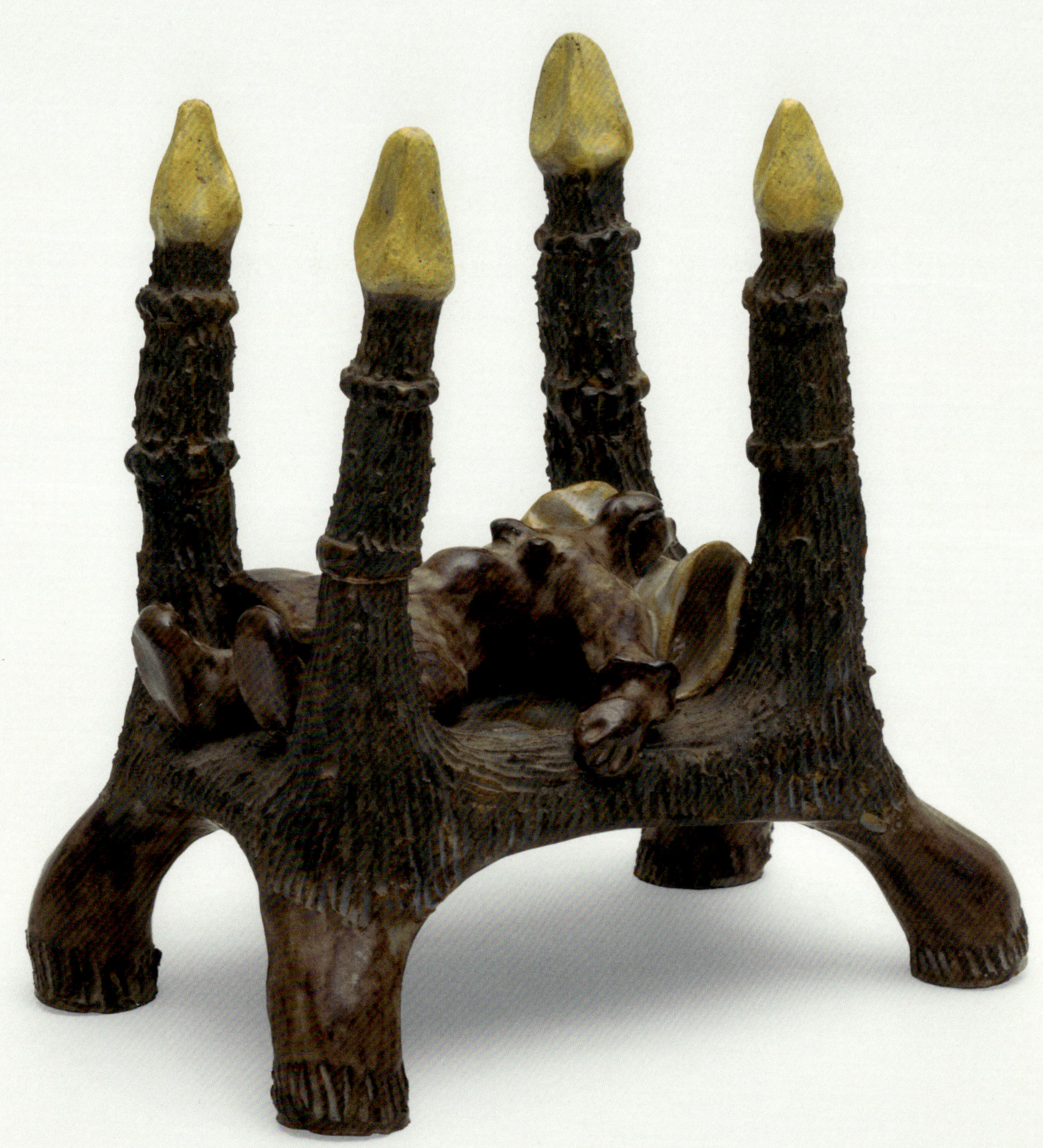

66   *Baldaquín* (Canopy Bed), 1971

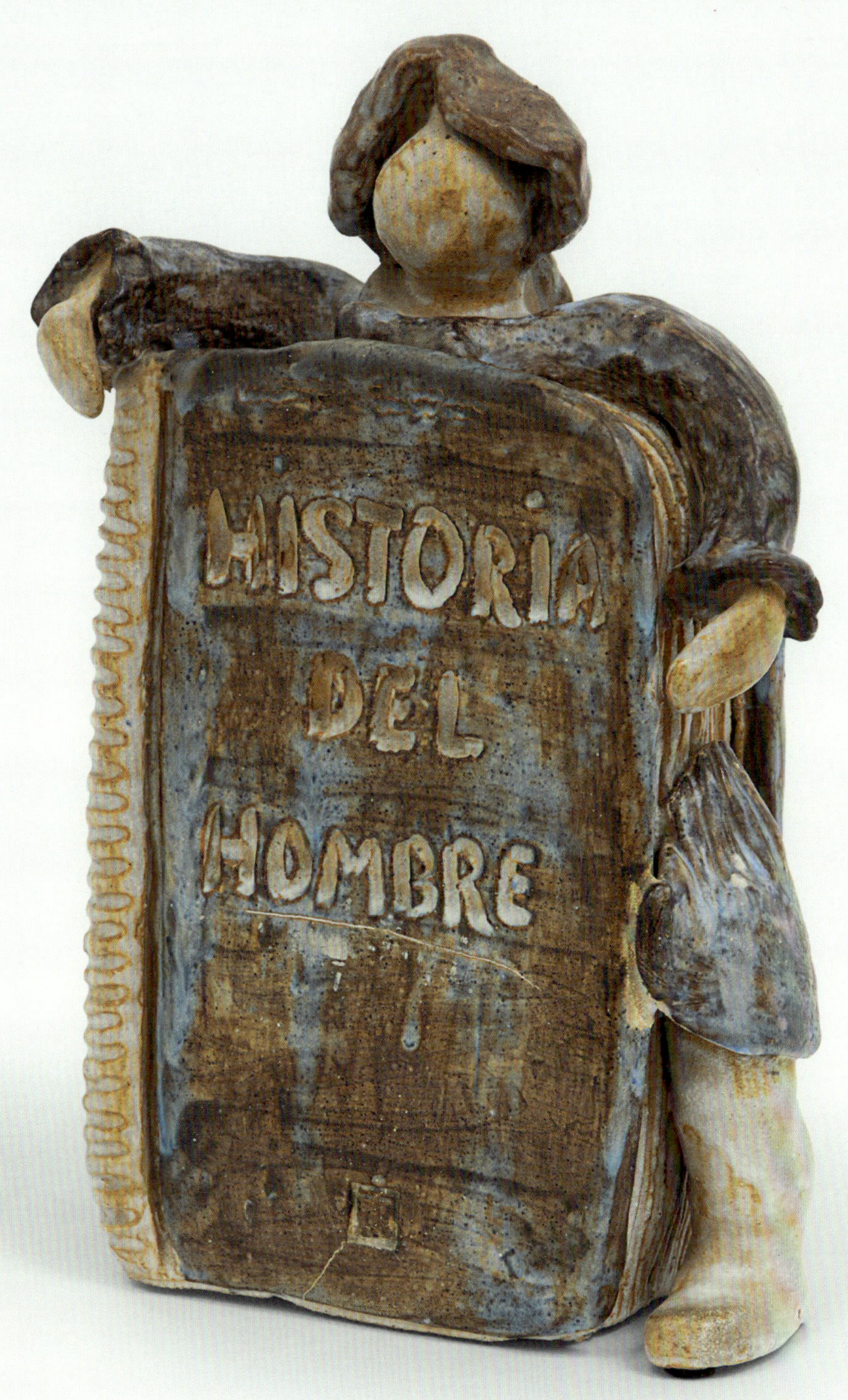

La mujer en la historia (Women in History), 1975   67

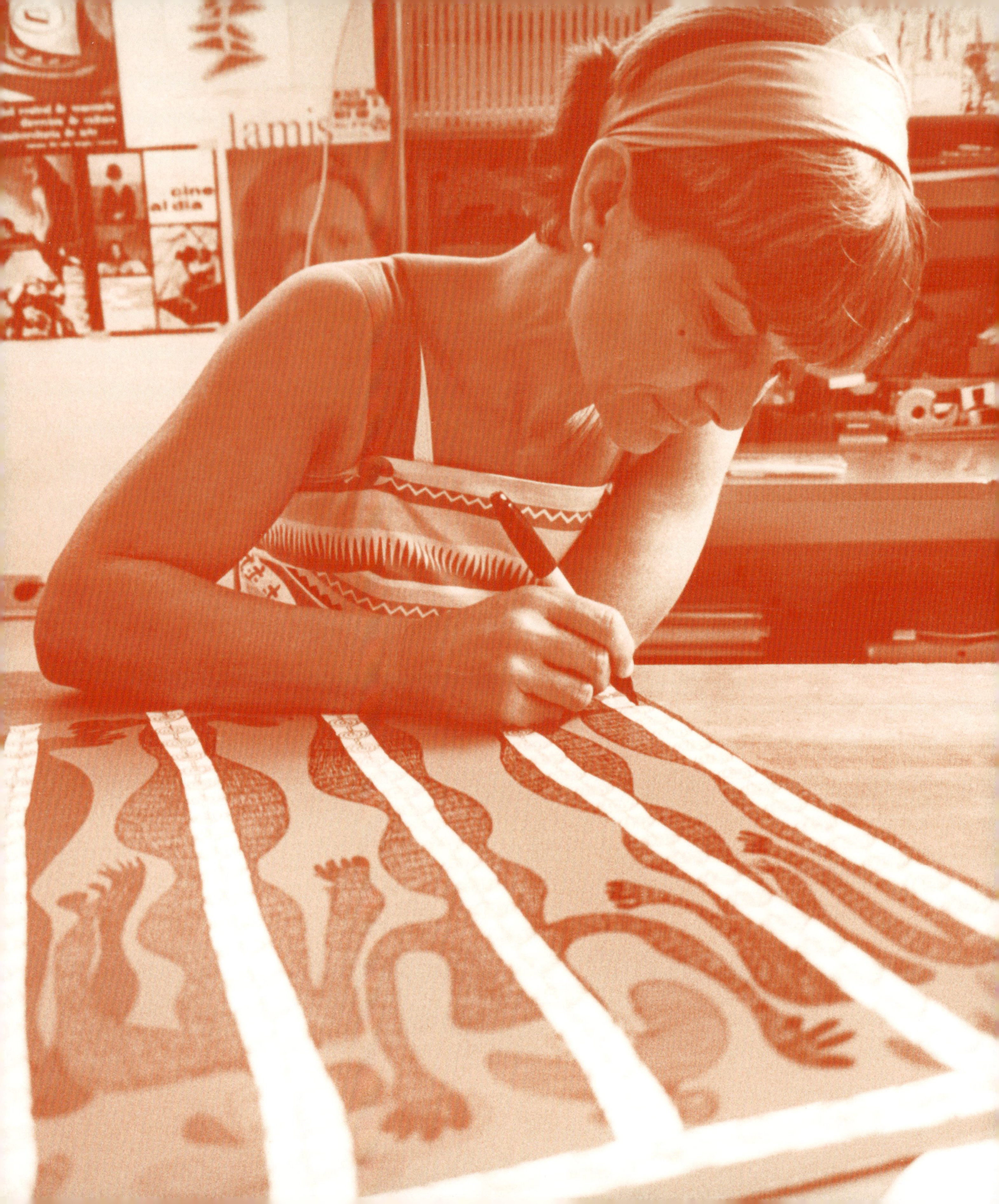

DRAWINGS

SELECTIONS FROM
THE *EVAS AL DESNUDO*
(NAKED EVES) SUITE, 1972

Más que unidas, entrelazadas
(More Intertwined than Joined)
¡Coño! (Cunt!)
La siguen (They Follow Her)
Tras el abanico (Behind the Fan)
La dulce espera (The Sweet Wait)
Parirás (You'll Deliver)
Como un Buda (Like a Buddha)
Tras el biombo (Behind the Screen)
La empollada (The Hatching)
Así empezó todo (Thus it all Began)
Reina yo¿ (Me, a Queen¿)
Mariposeando (Butterflying)
Los reproduce (She Reproduces Them)
Por aquí no! (Not Here!)
Femineidad (Femininity)

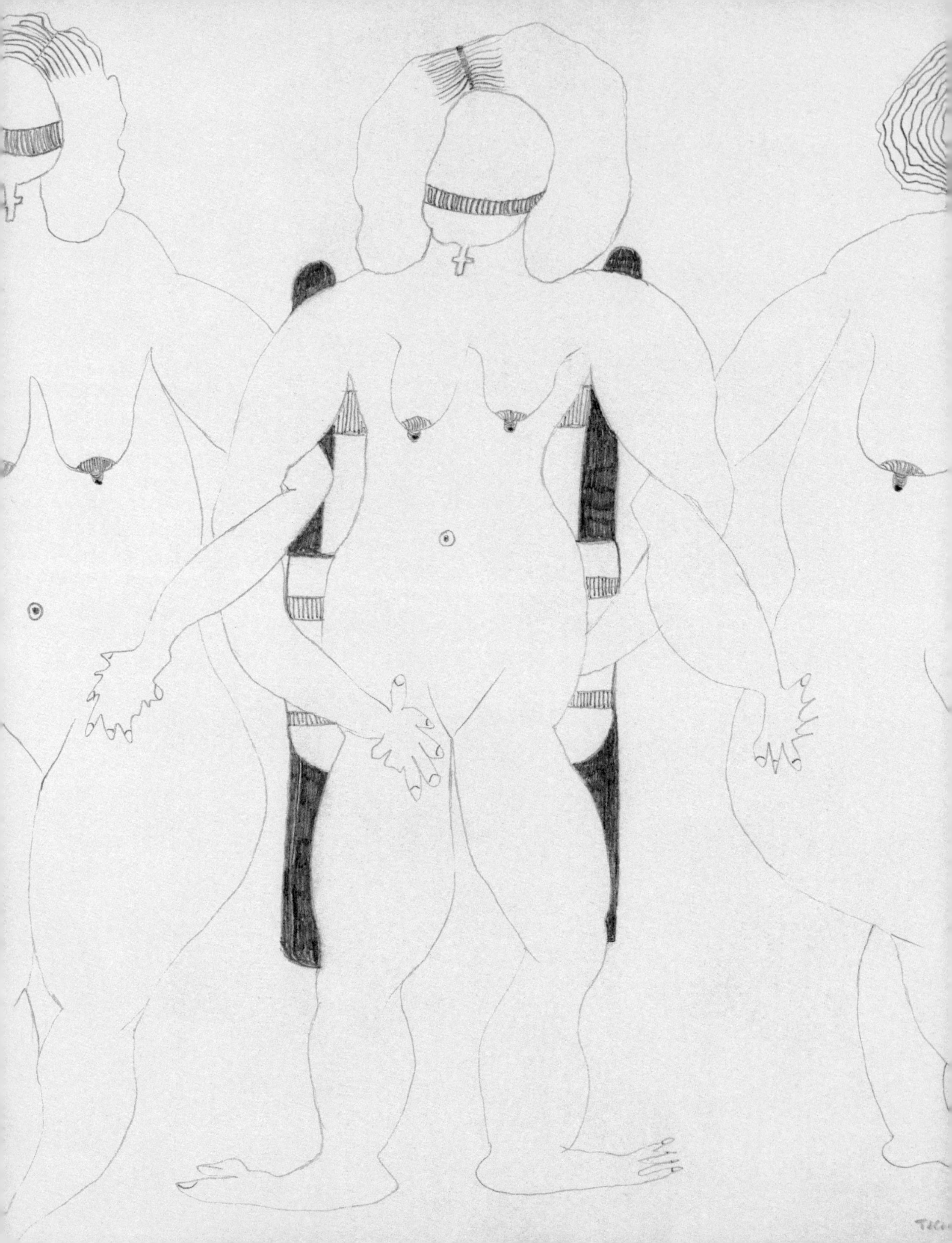

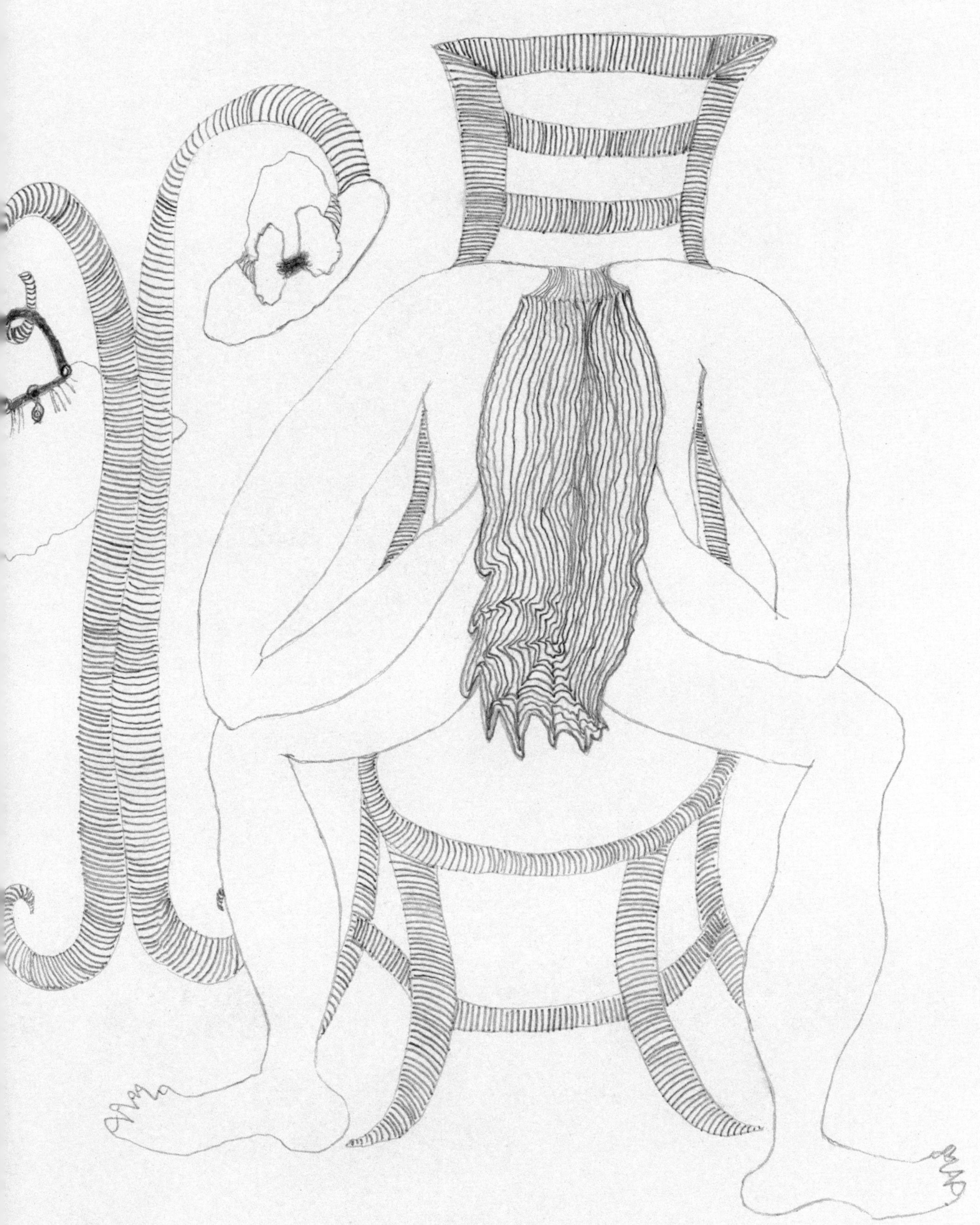

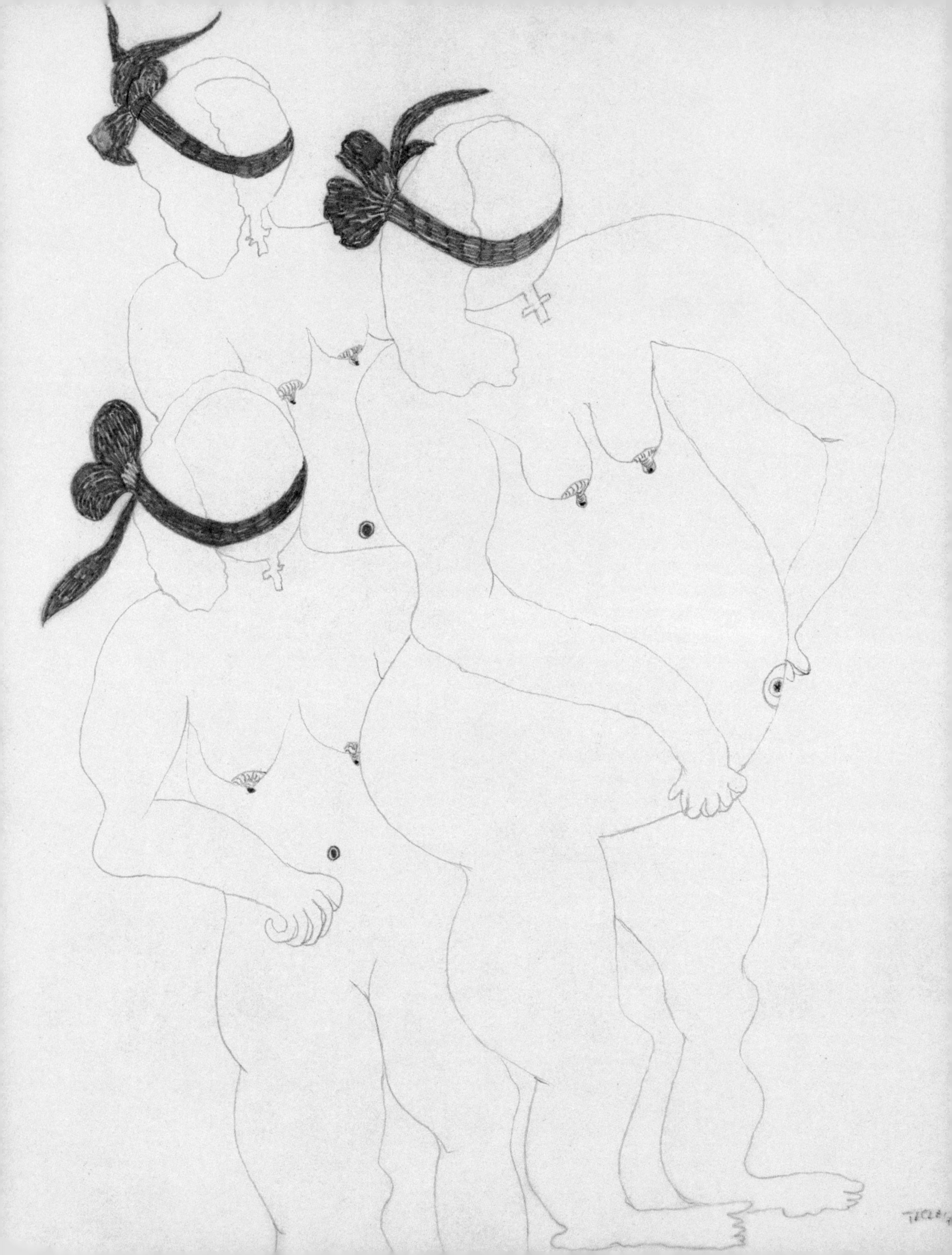

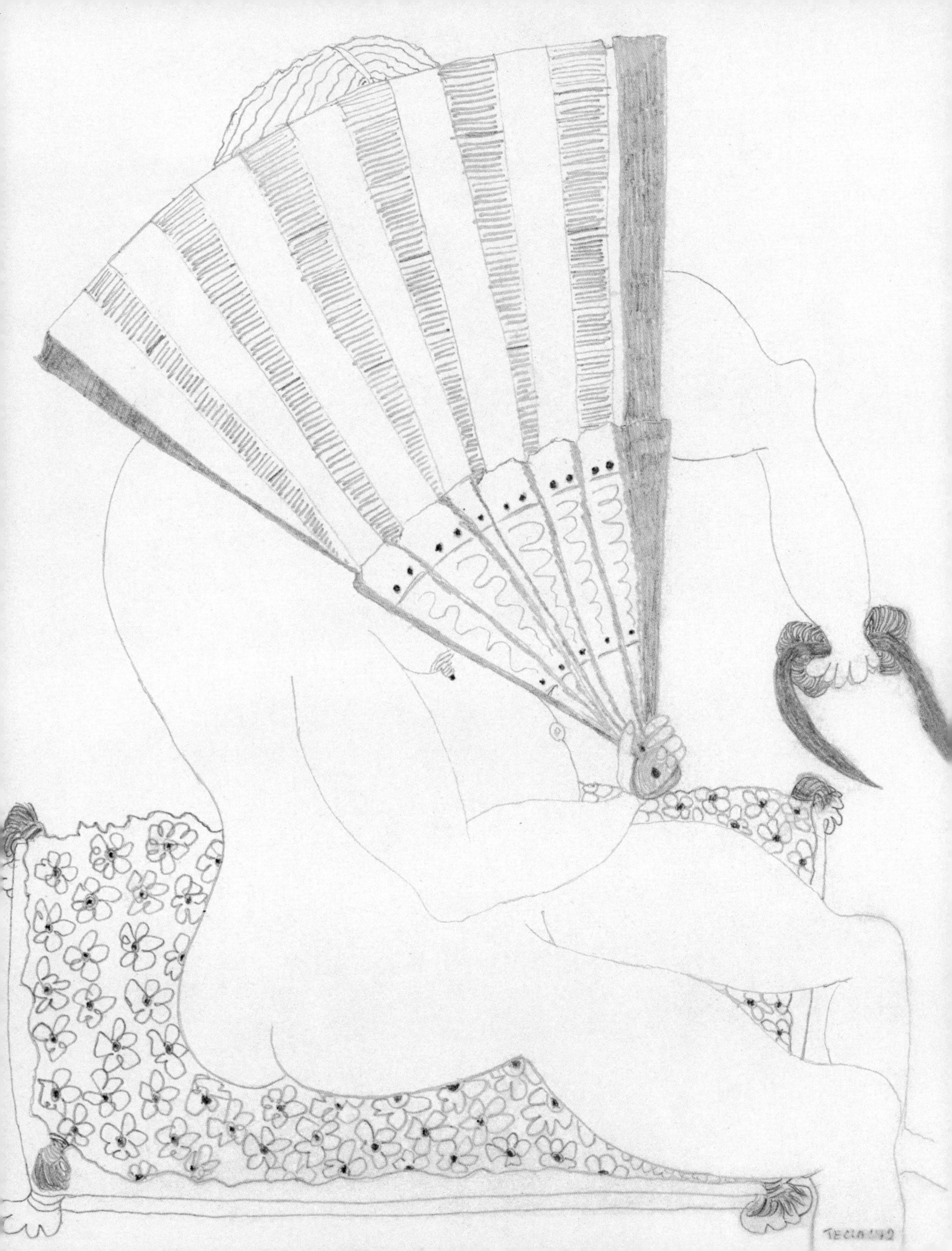

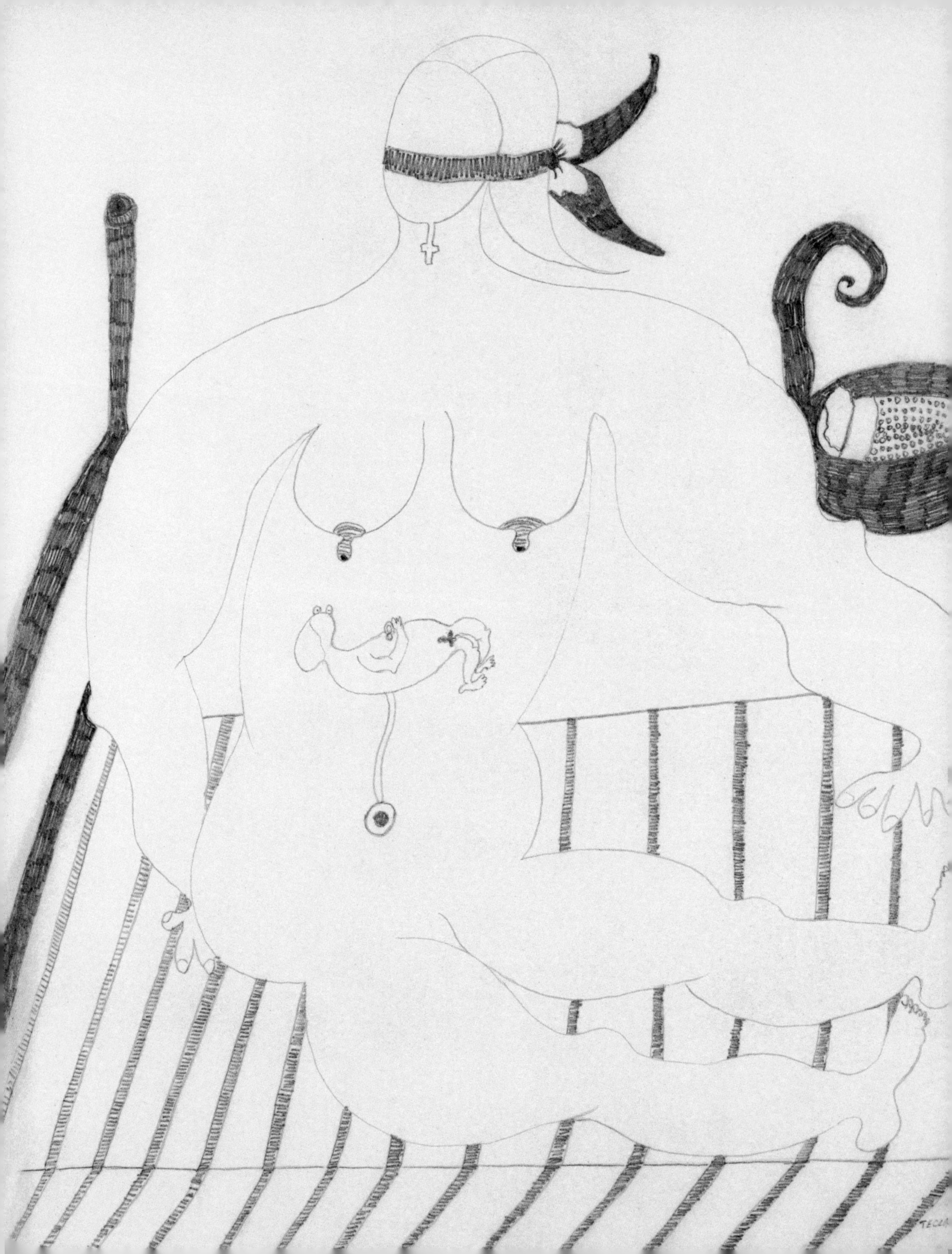

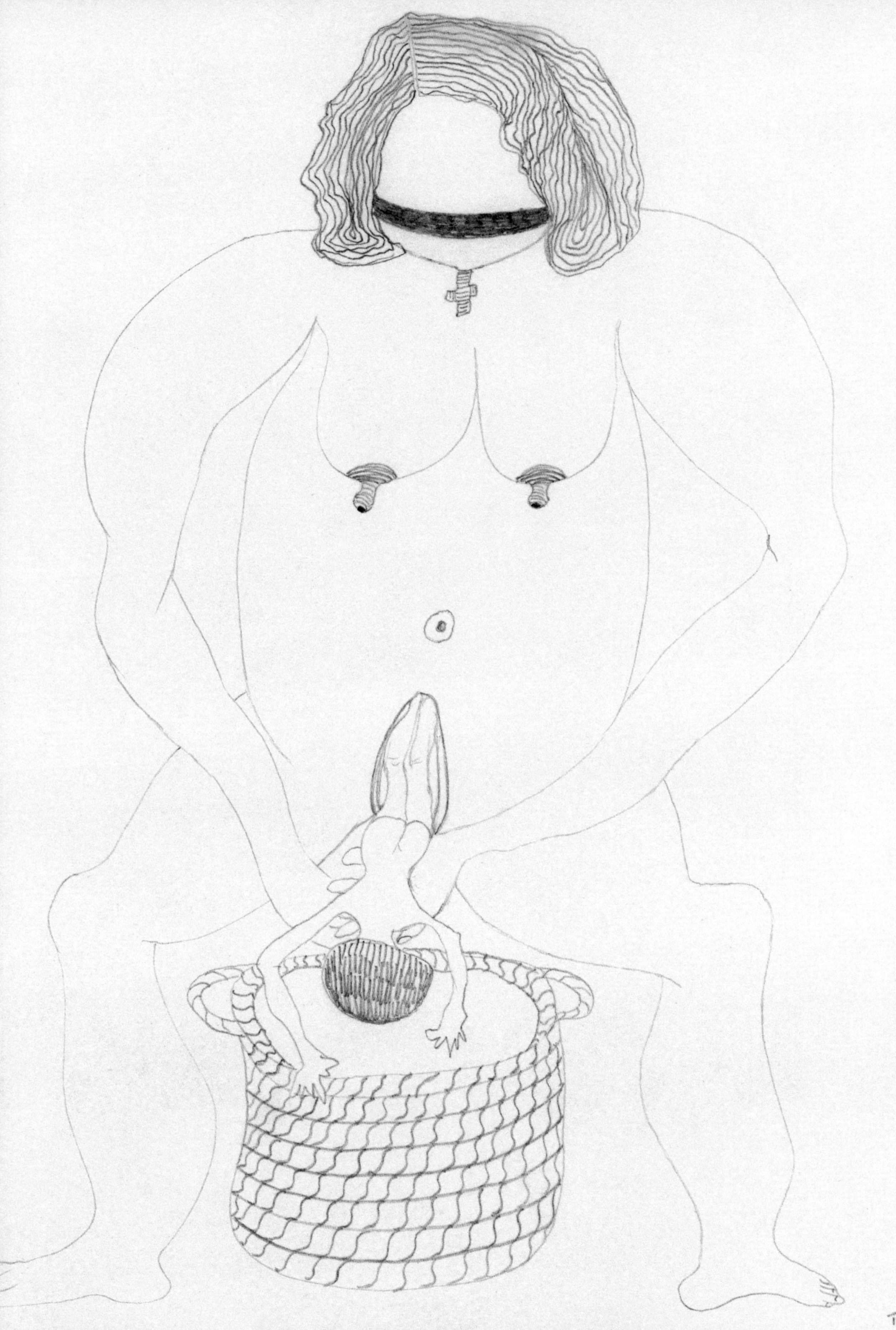

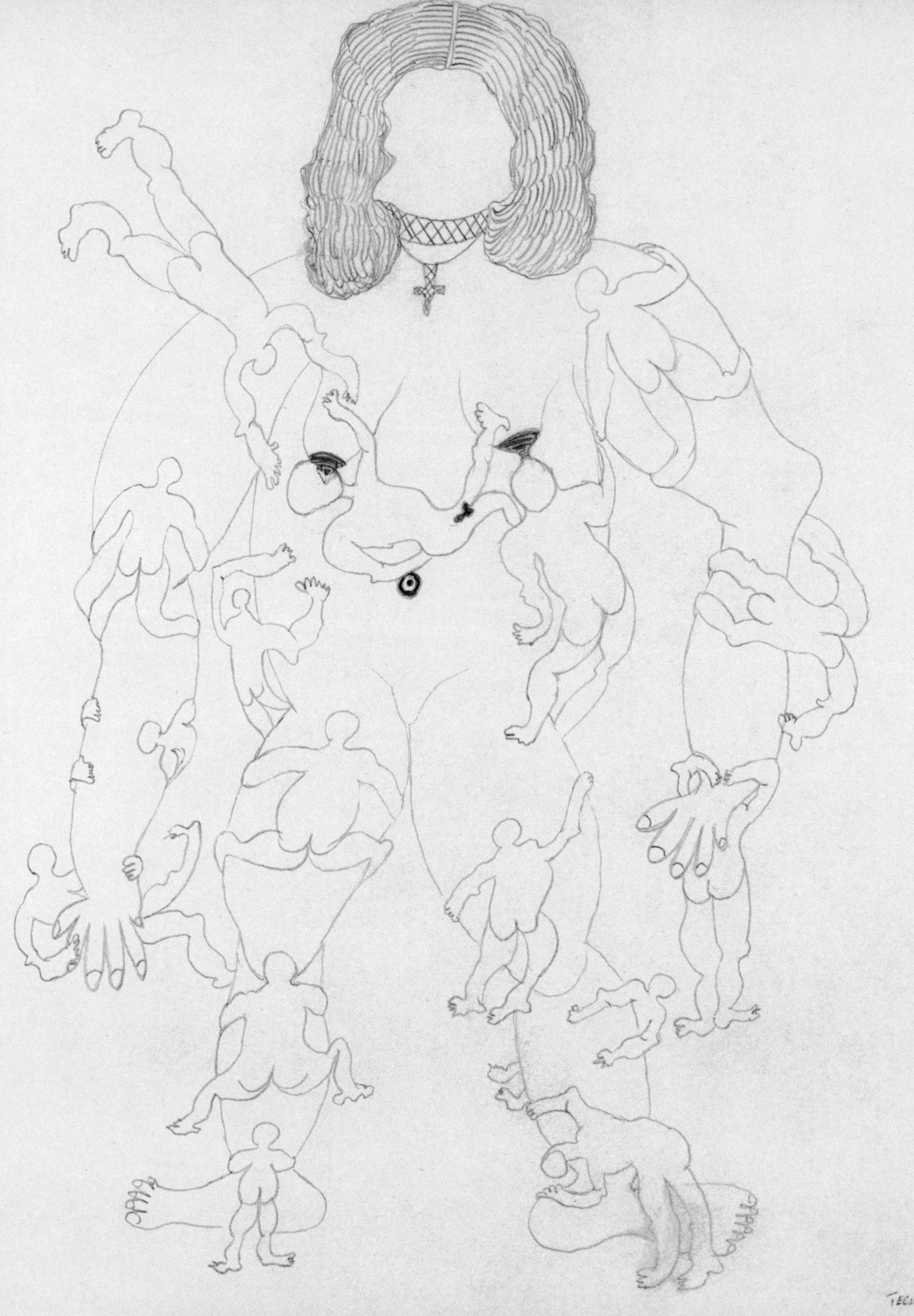

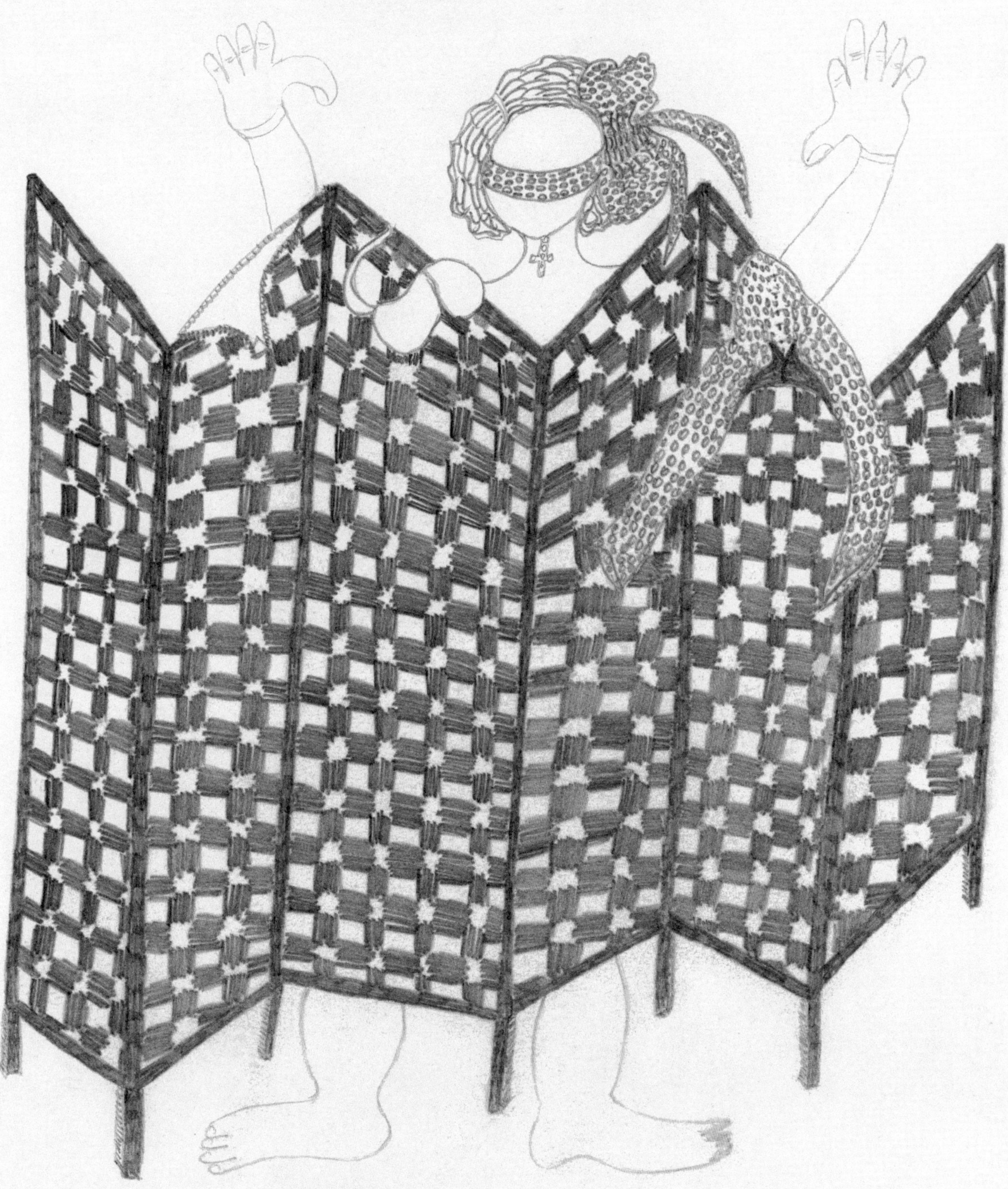

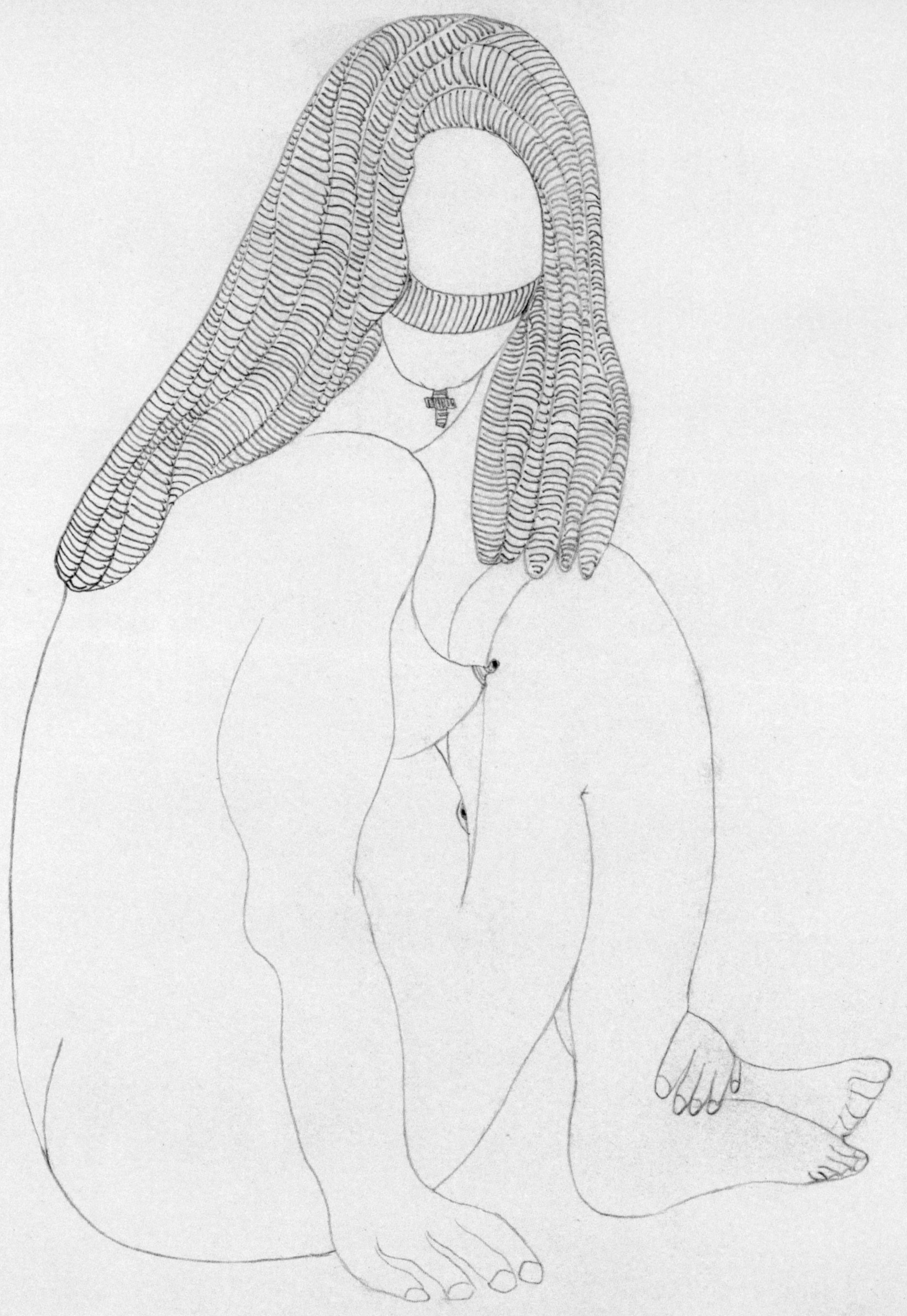

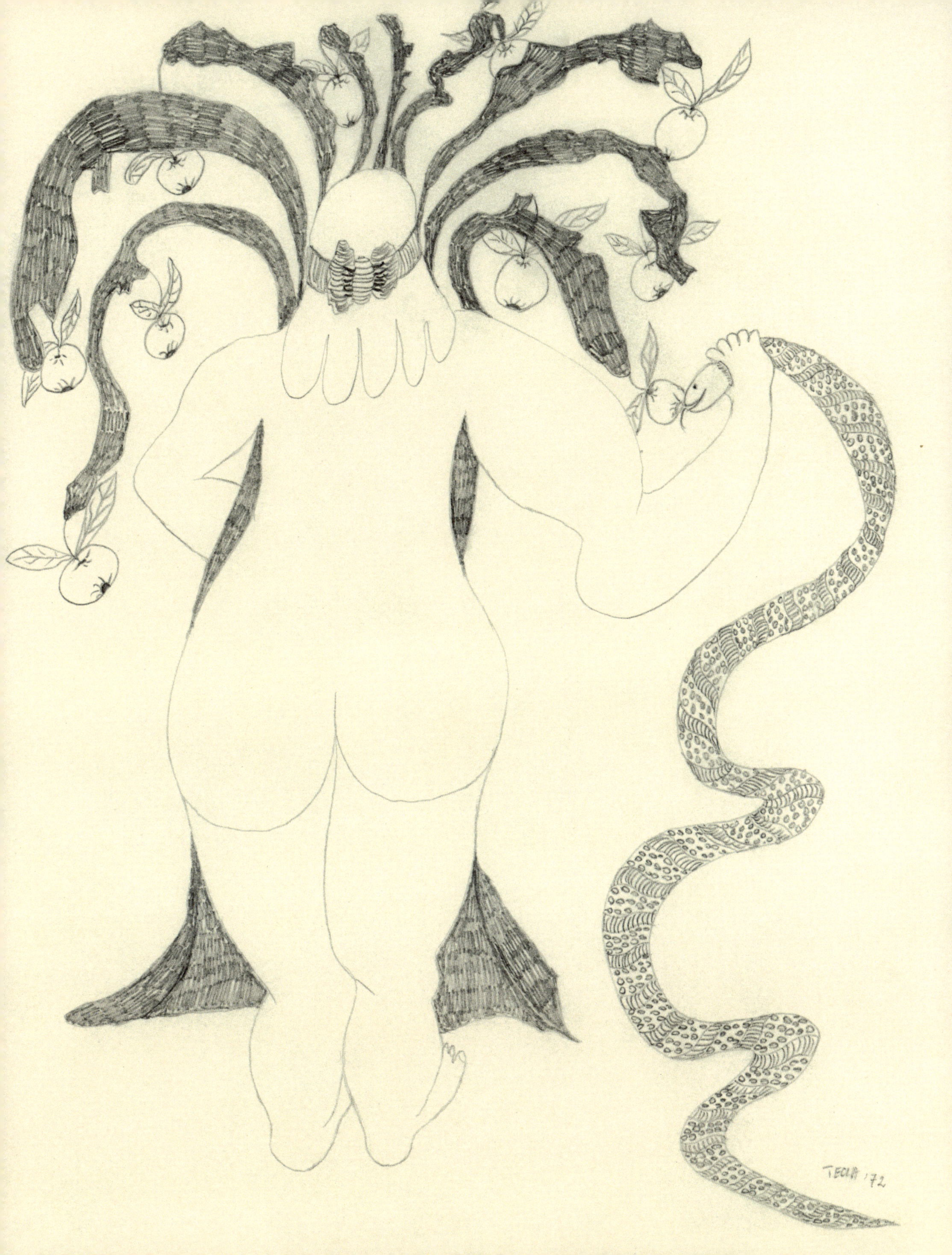

TECLA '72

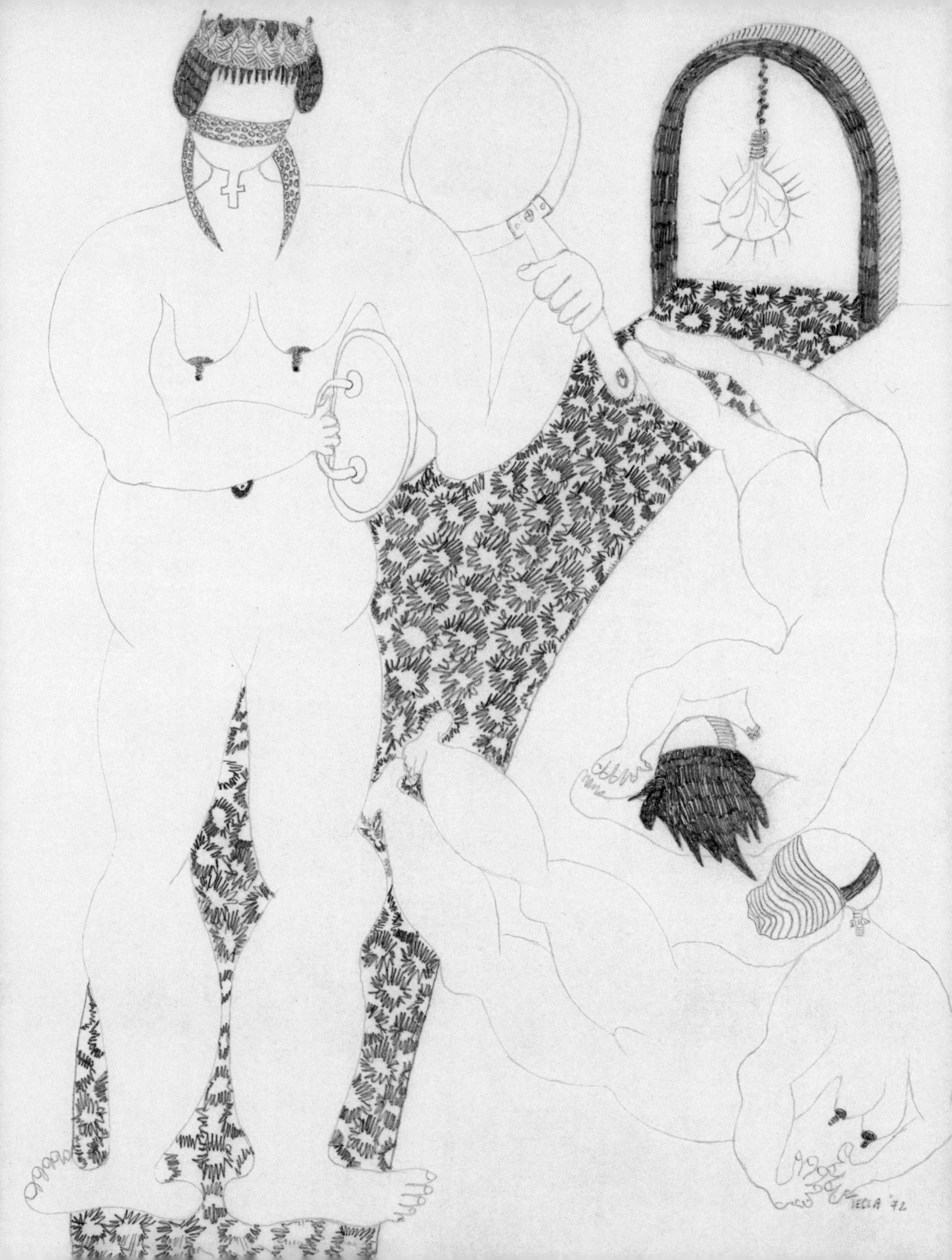

TECLA '72

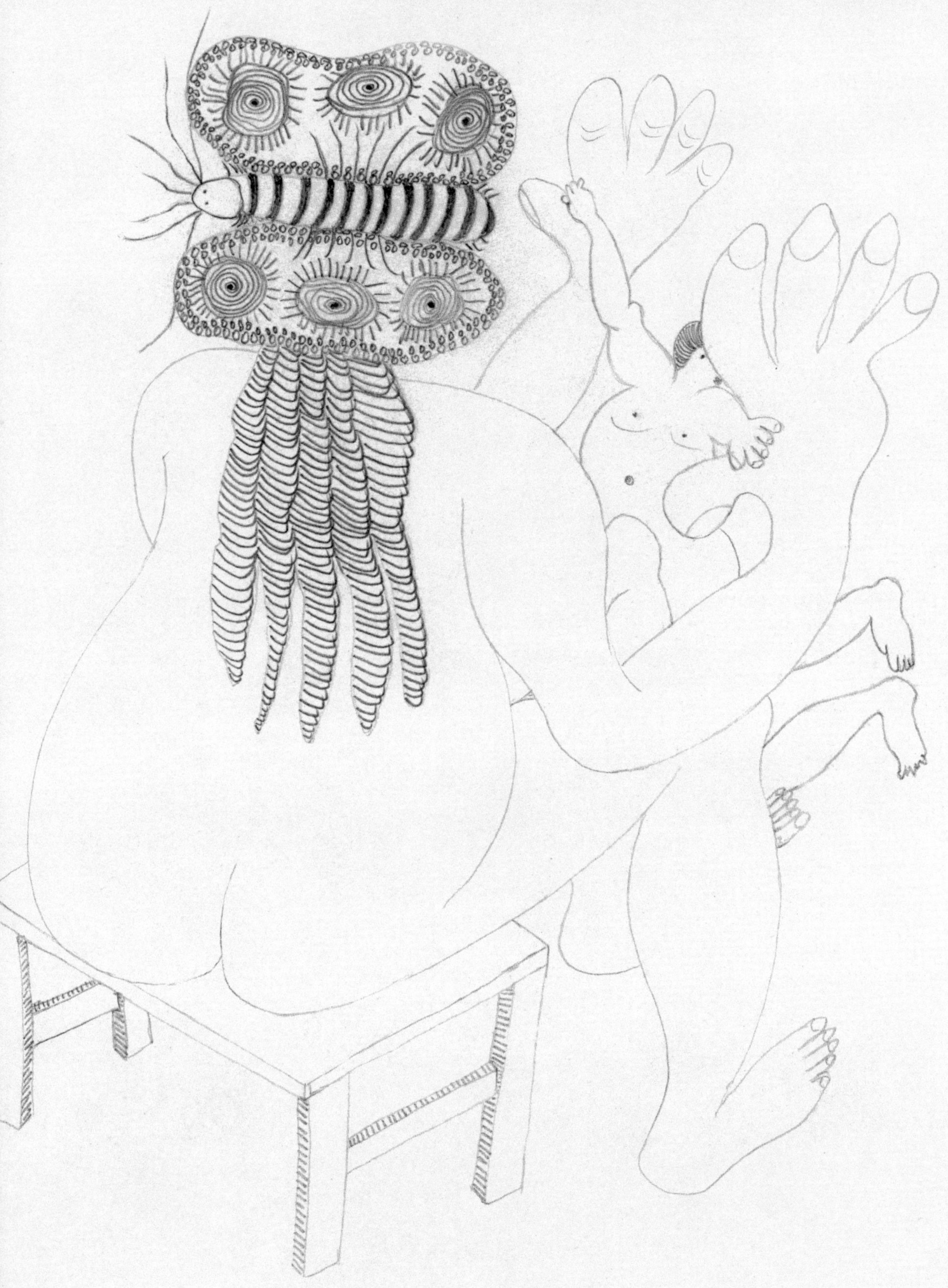
TECLA '72

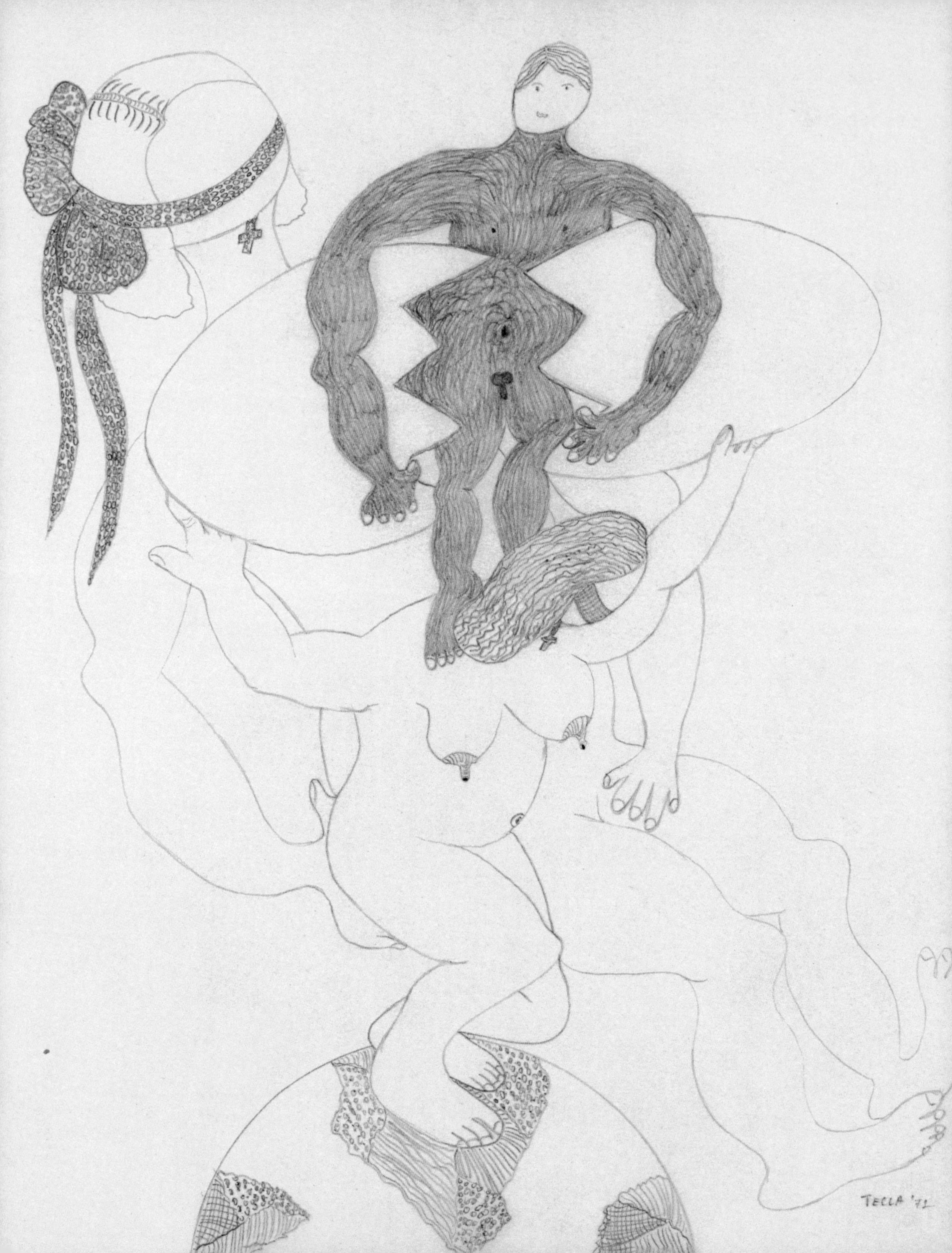
TECLA '72

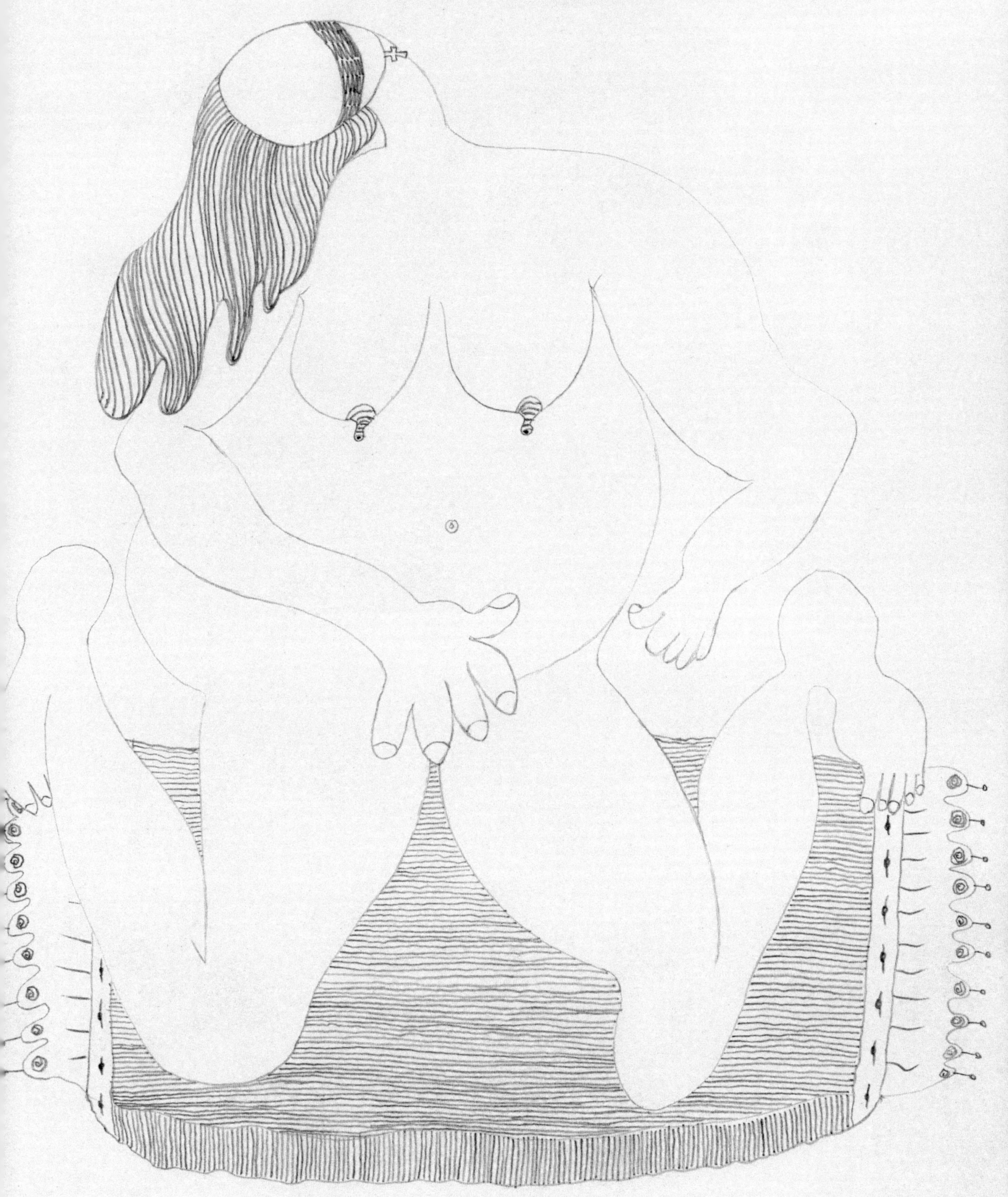

TECLA '72

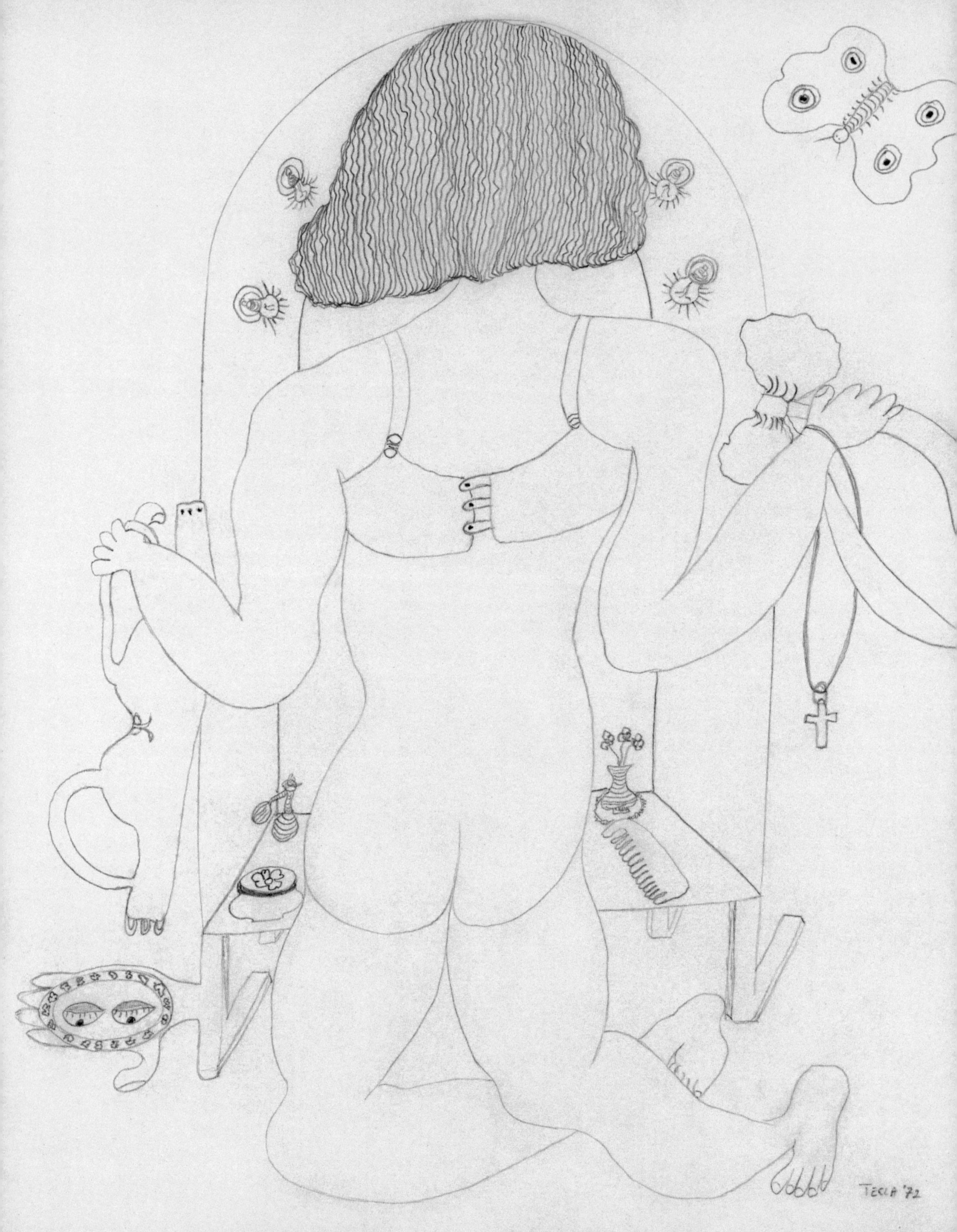

TECLA '72

WRITINGS

TRANSLATED BY
LUCÍA HINOJOSA GAXIOLA

4

Lasting
from infinite lapses
I end up
saying
that I'll last
despite
the battlements.

21

I hate
already I hate
my daughter's
dependency
her future oppression
her exploitation,
I hate already
her ephemeral beauty
her inherited fallacy
in thinking she can be another
I hate
already I hate
her amassed teachings
unconscious
I hate even more her possible clarity
if she becomes aware,
I hate already
her future frustration
her solitude
her inhibition
in complaint or dissatisfaction,
I hate already
her body's offering

virgin of initiation
the one raping her
believing he possesses her
I hate
already I hate
her fair and young hope
that thinks that love
can exist
without equal harmony
and parity,

I hate already
her transparent and pristine knowledge
the product of descendants' transferences
I hate
already I hate
her airy departure
in combat
that will withdraw her own self
I hate already
her vulnerable faith
in tomorrow
blurred in its overture,
more hate
if I didn't believe this with ardor,
I hate already
my predictions
and the inheritance I am leaving
in germs of struggles and rejections
this emergent and clear loneliness
without offering her
pleasure
or someone she can be with
truthfully
entirely intensely and as equals.

23

This body of mine
assemblage of flesh and bones
floating marrow
imprisoned
and the blood is irrigated
in between conduits of violet color.
Outwards

to the exterior
flesh
edgy almost always,
sometimes still.
Featherless
two abandoned wings
of open fingers and claws
hooks for prey and flight
Three parts manifested,
the center is in the middle
and upwards more than everything
my intense brain fluctuation
becoming mad behind eyes
eyelid-less
naked
extroverted
towards foreign images
that are mine.
Two pendular tangerines
without gravity
administered milk
distilling lullabies
lubricant baby bottles
of sensualities,
mother and daughter of another,

and myself.
Many cavities,
so many because of truth,
but only one centered
in the middle of the whole,
concave
stuck inwardly
timid vigil of breath
kaleidoscopic blazon of becoming,
submerged in visceral suburbs,

a timbre that oppresses
the gut
when it bloats
lacerated
according to the semen ingested
wanting or not to birth.
Between the legs,
Sustenance of preached paths,
The oyster is jealous
Peeled clam
Of remote pleasure,
humid
with blushed lapses
monthly
acid lymph
active and sensuous
in its bait
now it gathers itself
now it flourishes
mellow
behind the hairy defense of a cave
cubicle of amendment
and creation.
Counterweighting everything

separated in parts
two peaches of rest
(what do I want them for?)
seat buttocks,
white of gaze,
conduit of expulsion
and convergences of feces.

Epílogos (Caracas: Ediciones La Draga
y el Dragón, 1987).

Un día mi hijo me dijo: "A mi maestra no le gustan mis dibujos, porque dice que veo las cosas en no inventos míos y no como son en la realidad."
Recordé improvisamente que yo también fui niña y también a mi maestra no le gustaban mis dibujos por no ser la copia de los objetos, personas o animales. Aun cuando absurdo, creo que yo y mi hijo tuvimos la misma maestra.
Perdí el encanto de dibujar y me sentí obligada a una tarea desagradable y fastidiosa, con la misma sensación de cuando confesaba, de rodillas, tras una reja, mis pecados sin saber que fuera un peccato.
No lograba ver las cosas como quería las viera mi maestra y ella tampoco me enseñaba.
Encontré el remedio calcando figuras de libros y revistas.
Al reprimir mi fantasía, mi humor, mi visión de niña, creo que fui guardando adentro de mí, celosamente, la mágica aureola con la cual involucraba las cosas desde afuera, volviéndolas mi verdad.
Mas nunca dibujé porque me habían enseñado a no saber dibujar.
Lo reprimido, lo que guardamos adentro necesariamente debe desatarse algún día y, a los treinta y pico años de edad, sentí ganas de recordar las flores, la gente, los animales, las plazas, la playa, mis compañeras y las mismas palabras que no entendía, así como yo

quería y no como habían pretendido enseñarme a verlas.
El recuerdo que yo guardaba de ellas logró hacerme descubrir las pequeñas verdades de las cuales están constituidas las cosas, encerradas en aquella aureola que era mía y que sigue siendo mía, ingenua o tremenda, aún bajo la transformación que los años alimentaron.

Tecla

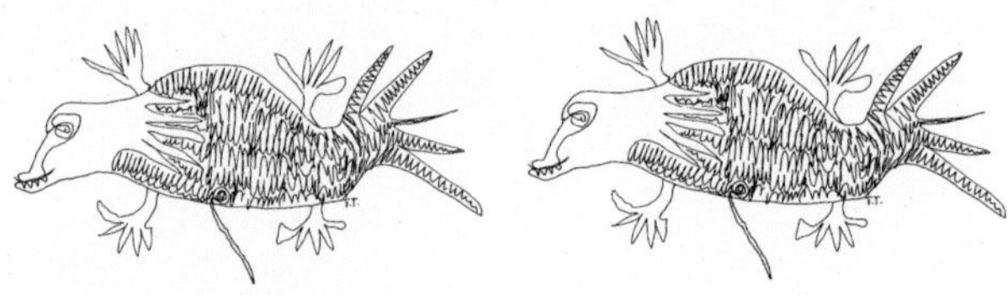

Tecla Tofano's writing as published in the catalogue for her drawings exhibition,
Dibujos de Tecla Tofano (Tecla Tofano's Drawings), Galería El Pez Dorado, Caracas, 1965

I'm not very keen on lectures and even less—as in this case, when I've thought it necessary to explain some things that do not only belong to me—that another introduces me. I think this owes an explanation, not for the critics, if there are any for that matter, but rather and for much more important reasons to me, for the gallery and museum visitors, the buyers and those interested in ceramics.

To clarify: first of all I don't believe in applied arts, major arts, or minor arts. I also don't believe I am resolving a sculptural problem. If for some the three-dimensional is obligatory and sculpturally necessary, the problem is reduced to a personal question.

Matter obliges me and limits me, that's why I'm making ceramics. For me (and if I am mistaken, I am so with conviction), I make ceramics in spite of forms, in order not to betray the clay. Forms are only the means of expression, and in this way they're felt. I'm interested in design as long as it serves what I want to say. If baroque, if jumbled, if not pleasant to the gaze, if distasteful some of the time, it is because what I'm seeking to express is not pretty.

I'm not interested in absolute definitions. I don't believe in "-isms" or in traditional ceramics (if I'd believe, I would say, because of how little I know of ceramics, that the "sculptural" tendency is the most antique and most traditional). Everything I said before could appear as justifications; maybe they're needed. More than anything I want to clarify for those who appreciate ceramics that sometimes my materials or my "aesthetic" presentations are not the most pleasant. There are mistakes; I have problems. I work with the worst clay that exists (clay from San Antonio for pots), and sometimes I use higher than this clay can resist with the goal of achieving qualities and "ceramics."

Forms sometimes distort matter (clay, fire, varnish); therefore, they produce ruptures. I seek to correct them. I've succeeded in dominating the "faults" of what's possible. I can't make sculpture. I'm still making ceramics. I haven't abandoned the potter's wheel, and I am not planning on doing it. But my expressive necessities turn me back to modeling—this is the word.

I'm still making ceramics, including the present possibility of doubt that tomorrow I might feel it necessary to take another expressive modality that allows me to say something else or something different. I will decide and accept it.

De la silla a la cápsula, catalogue text.
(Caracas: Sala Mendoza, 1969).

Shall I ask myself why my ceramics are not only pots? Sometimes I understand myself and answer myself. I reflect in order to find some answers when necessary. I don't feel I've distanced myself—in the real sense of the word—from anything. Rather I feel closer to all my old forms (I don't know up to what point they were habitual or traditional or functional), and I feel that this today is exactly a by-product of them. A medium, among many, of expression. A possibility of saying something else that belongs to me—intimate and from/for everyone—in the search for more formal freedom with a material that allows me to employ it in its plasticity, in its boiling hardness and final product. I'm not against anything or nothing; I'm just admitting the possibility of demonstrating that I can use and take advantage of this field of expression without altering or changing the primary elements that are used as often for pots as for modeling sculpture or ceramics.

If I don't alter or change the material and it resists, it means I am making ceramics, even if the formal expression changes.

Change is determined—more than by material or by form—by my attitude, my expressive necessity, and by the possibility of saying something different from what a pot, a dish, or a concentric container could oblige me to say. I believe that being forced or feeling only the strictly functional or belonging to everyday necessities wouldn't be an adequate and honest response to my possibilities, forcing me into one and unique problem that is not even completely and exclusively responding to the necessities of my studio and my technical knowledge. I don't evade it, but I restrict it for practical reasons. Why limit ourselves? I seek to tell and say more about myself, of the world I live in, not only giving the view of a single material in objects that will be used very little, as in truly functional objects, deformed for the sake of pure decoration.

Hands give what my body, my mind, and my knowledge couldn't do or give without fingers.

When I've mistakenly searched for the alteration of matter, I've had losses, destruction, and with this I've learned matter's own limitations, and because of these same losses and limitations I've gotten to know real possibilities that I've taken advantage of in relation to one's expression. Until this equilibrium between myself and matter is governed, I will keep making sculpture, and if that relationship has to be broken, I'll search for another path. Modeling is not new in ceramic history. I maintain that it is not sculpture as long as the objective is contained in the problem concerning matter and its limitations and that this mustn't deprive the author. The day such boundary is crossed, consciously or unconsciously, matter itself will be the index and evident signal of this leap: its destruction.

My experience—years of research, failures and achievements, maturity, life, questions and answers, the capacity and need for expression—can consolidate the work in the same sense or it could provoke the need for a new expressive experience.

I am the one that lives through transformations; therefore, I don't perceive abrupt changes but its aftermath.

Any question arises from exterior pressures about oneself.

The modeled object has mystery. The pot is clear, logical; it explains itself. Its interiority corresponds exactly to its exteriority.

The concentric walls around an empty cavity can't hide or deprive its interior knowledge. The air locked is free. Matter is known in its totality. There is no mystery.

The solid object—sturdy, modeled—presents only its exterior form and hides in its gut what is not visible.

The matter that has become prisoner in its interior, what is unknown to its own creator, didn't have any motives to break free or enough strength to explode.

This mystery perhaps grants me the stimuli to keep seeking clarity without its obvious possession, and this is what leaves me with hope that I might know tomorrow something that I don't know today.

Tecla Tofano, "Reflections," Artist's testimony, *Revista Nacional de Cultura* (Caracas, 1967).

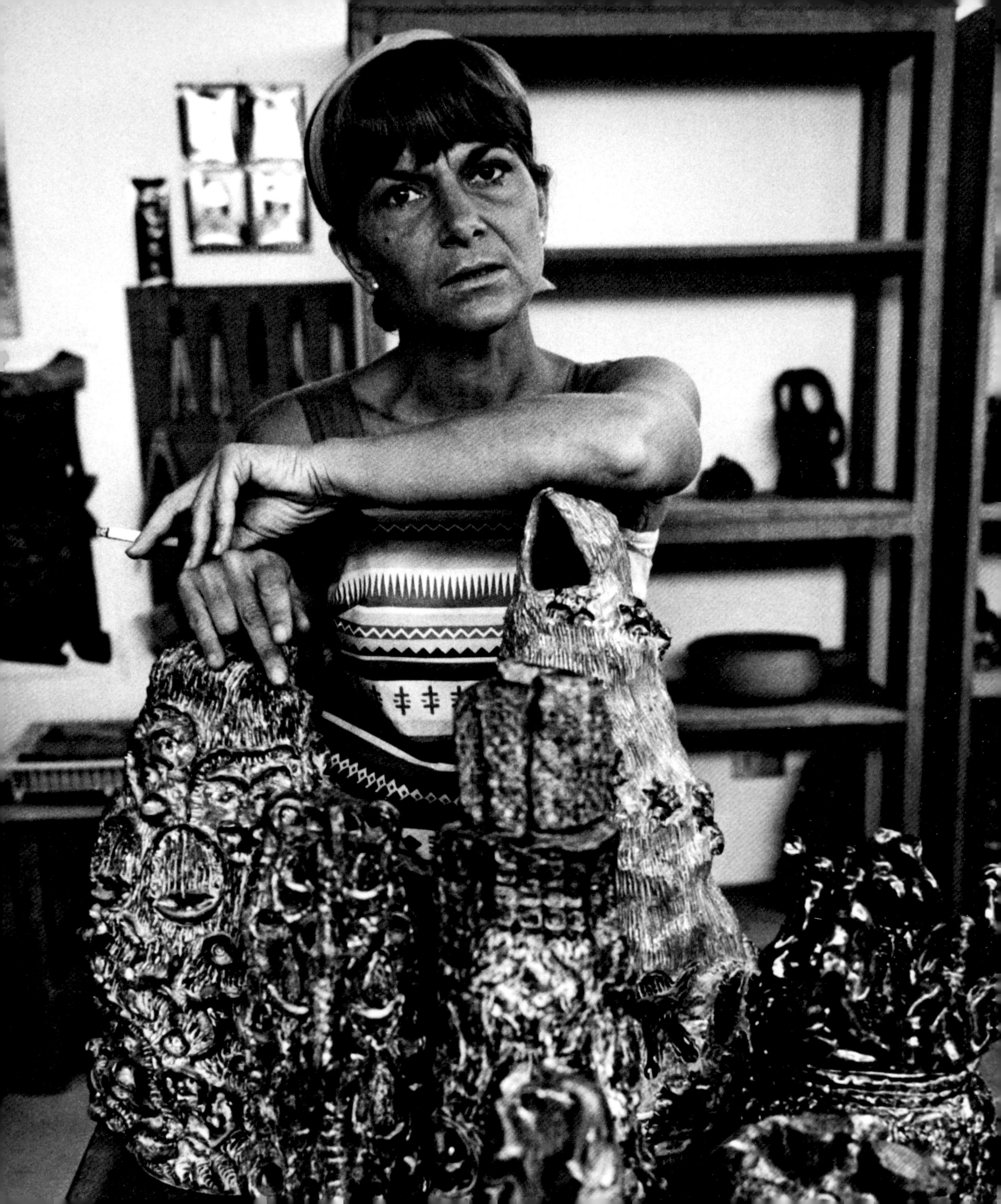

CHRONOLOGY

LUIS FELIPE FARÍAS S.

1927 Tecla Tofano Sessa is born on March 5 in Naples, Italy, to Italian parents. She is the third of five children.

Her mother, Rafaella Sessa, raised in a privileged family, studied singing and piano before marrying her father, Nicola Tofano, a successful lawyer with progressive ideas. Her father died when she was only ten years old, causing a difficult financial blow and prompting her mother to move them to Rome in search of better opportunities.

1951 In Rome, she meets Venezuelan economist Armando Córdova, who is finishing his postgraduate studies before returning to his country. They fall in love and get married [FIG. 1].

1952 She arrives in Venczuela at the age of twenty-four. The couple settles in San Antonio de Los Altos, a neighborhood of Caracas. When asked about her life there, Tofano replied:

I loved everything about Venezuela, having arrived in the middle of the Pérez Jiménez dictatorship. Caracas was almost bucolic, not like today, a very violent and dangerous city. Of course, by then I encountered macho traits, but in no way worse than those of any other country, since this is a worldwide problem with various forms of manifestation.[1]

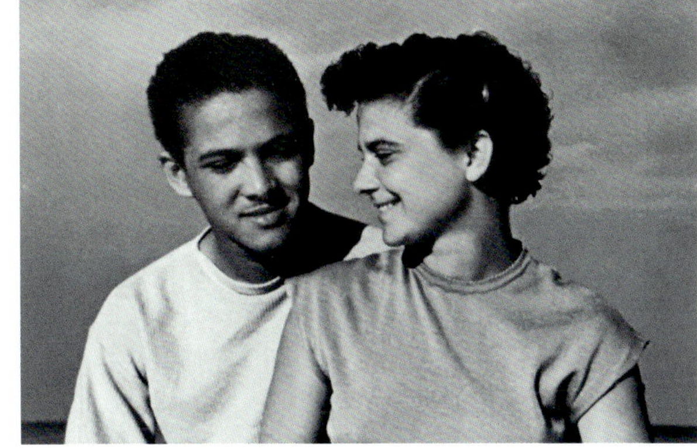

FIG. 1. Tecla Tofano and Armando Córdova, 1952

Unlike her family, the young Tofano forges a strong connection with socialist movements, both in Italy and Venezuela. After arriving in Venezuela, she immediately becomes involved in the activities of the incipient left wing of the fifties. There, she will develop activism, dissemination, and support for her feminist ideals.

She gives birth to her daughter, Lucia Córdova Tofano.

1954 For three years, she studies with Professor Miguel Arroyo at Taller de Esmaltes y Cerámica de la Escuela de Artes Plásticas y Aplicadas de Caracas (Enamel and Ceramic Workshop of the School of Plastic and Applied Arts of Caracas).

Tecla Tofano in her workshop, 1968

Cristina Merchán and Reina Herrera are among those studying alongside Tofano. She describes her early days at the school:

With the help of dear friends like Alejandro Otero, Sarita Mendoza, and Miguel Arroyo, I entered the Escuela de Artes Plásticas y Aplicadas de Caracas. Wanting to be an artisan was my intention. I did not need to understand the language during lessons taught by Miguel Arroyo, because the teaching of wheel throwing and the gestures of his hands were more eloquent than his words. In him there was a dynamic force of transmission for ceramics.[2]

Miguel Arroyo creates the Forma Veinte (Form Twenty) cooperative, aiming to promote ceramics, enamel, and handmade textiles. Ceramists Tofano and Merchán will participate in the venture, along with Mercedes Pardo, Alejandro Otero, Benjamín Mendoza, Sarita Guardia de Mendoza, and Argenis Madriz.

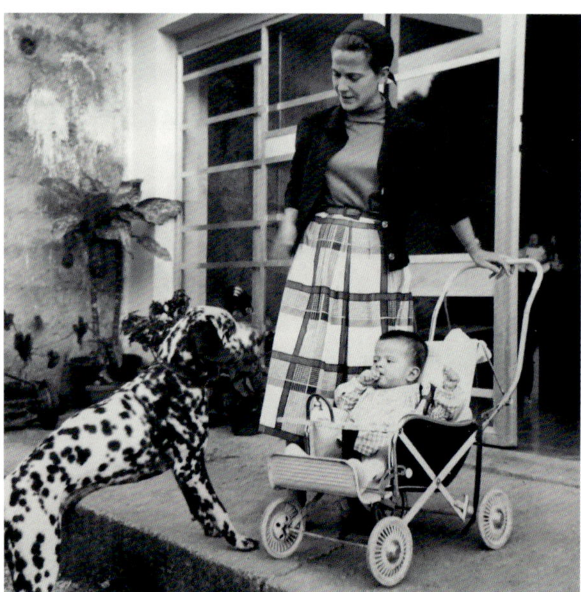

FIG. 2. Tecla Tofano and her son, Daniel, with the Guardia family's dalmatian, 1956

1955 She gives birth to her son, Daniel Córdova Tofano [FIG. 2].

1956 Her ceramics are shown for the first time in a group exhibition of works by students of the Escuela de Artes Plásticas y Aplicadas de Caracas.

At the end of the year, the school opens an exhibition with works by Cristina Merchán and Tofano. Their professor and curator Miguel Arroyo writes about their work:

If for Cristina Merchán, the form and the enamel with all its mystery are fundamental, for Tecla Tofano the texture is perhaps the most important. Her sgraffitos are now, more than linear ornamentation, traces of the different instruments with which she makes incisions in the clay to modify its appearance. This severity, together with the richness of the incising, gives an almost aggressive force to her ceramics.[3]

1957 During the next five years (1957–61), she participates in the Salón Oficial Anual de Arte Venezolano (Annual Official Salon of Venezuelan Art) at the Museo de Bellas Artes de Caracas.

Her daughter Lucia is hit by a car and tragically dies at the age of five.

1958 The dictatorship of Marcos Pérez Jiménez is overthrown by the Venezuelan National Armed Forces.

Tofano wins the National Prize of Applied Arts at the XIX Salón Oficial Anual de Arte Venezolano (XIX Annual Official Venezuelan Art Salon), Museo de Bellas Artes, Caracas, with her collection of utilitarian ceramics of varied and distinctive surfaces [FIG. 3].

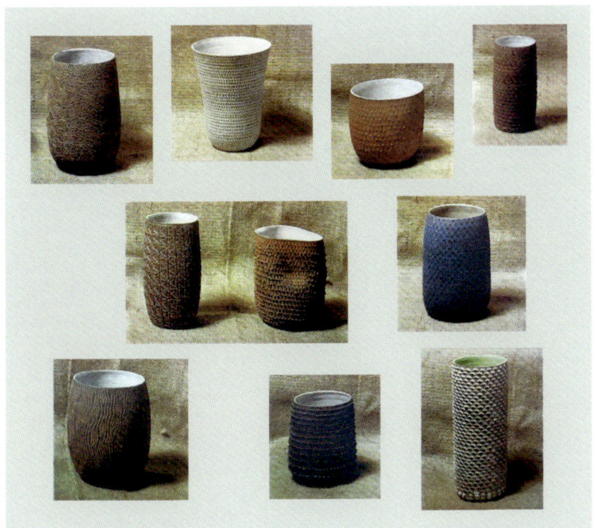

FIG. 3. Tecla Tofano's group of ceramics awarded the National Prize of Applied Arts at the XIX Salón Oficial Anual de Arte Venezolano, Museo de Bellas Artes, Caracas, 1958

She divorces Armando Córdova.

Participates in the exhibition *Pinturas, esculturas y cerámicas* (Paintings, Sculptures, and Ceramics) organized by the Venezuelan Pavilion at the International Fair of Brussels, Belgium.

Her work is included in *Cerámicas, esmaltes y vidrios* (Ceramics, Enamels, and Stained Glass), an exhibition organized by the gallery Sala Mendoza, Caracas—a private institution that has strongly supported the Venezuelan ceramics movement since 1957 by promoting and disseminating the work of the most relevant artists in the fired arts.

Tofano is appointed professor of artistic and architectural expression at the Faculty of Architecture of the Universidad Central de Venezuela (UCV), a position she held for twenty-five years until her retirement in 1983.

After the fall of Pérez Jiménez's dictatorship, she joins Venezuela's Communist Party.

1959 As the new leader of Cuba, Fidel Castro visits Venezuela on the first anniversary of the military uprising against Pérez Jiménez. He delivers a speech at UCV [FIG. 4].

Tecla Tofano: Cerámica (Ceramics) is the first solo exhibition dedicated to a ceramist at the Museo de Bellas Artes, Caracas. Tofano presents seventy-three utilitarian ceramics and eighteen silver and ceramic pieces of jewelry. Miguel Arroyo, curator of the show, elaborates on the artist's creative process:

These are exceptional pieces due to their boldness, sobriety, and economy of means. There is a deliberate exclusion of color and an emphasis on textures and monochromatic tones that accentuate the strength of the shapes. This is certainly the main virtue and the most singular characteristic of Tofano's work. Both her search and her findings are totally different from any other production, and the expressiveness that she wants to give to her vessels, that refined elementality, she completely achieves it.[4]

Her work is part of the exhibition *Veinte años del Salón a través de sus premios* (Twenty Years of the Salon and Its Awards), Museo de Bellas Artes, Caracas.

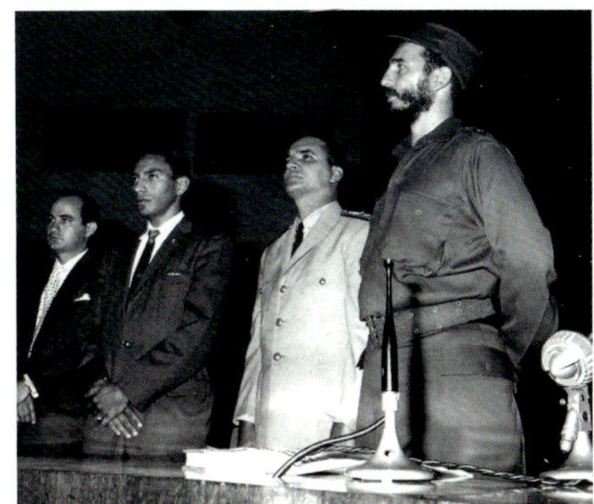

FIG. 4. Jesús Sanoja Hernandez, Jesús Carmona, Wolfgang Larrazábal and Fidel Castro at UCV's Aula Magna, Caracas January, 1959

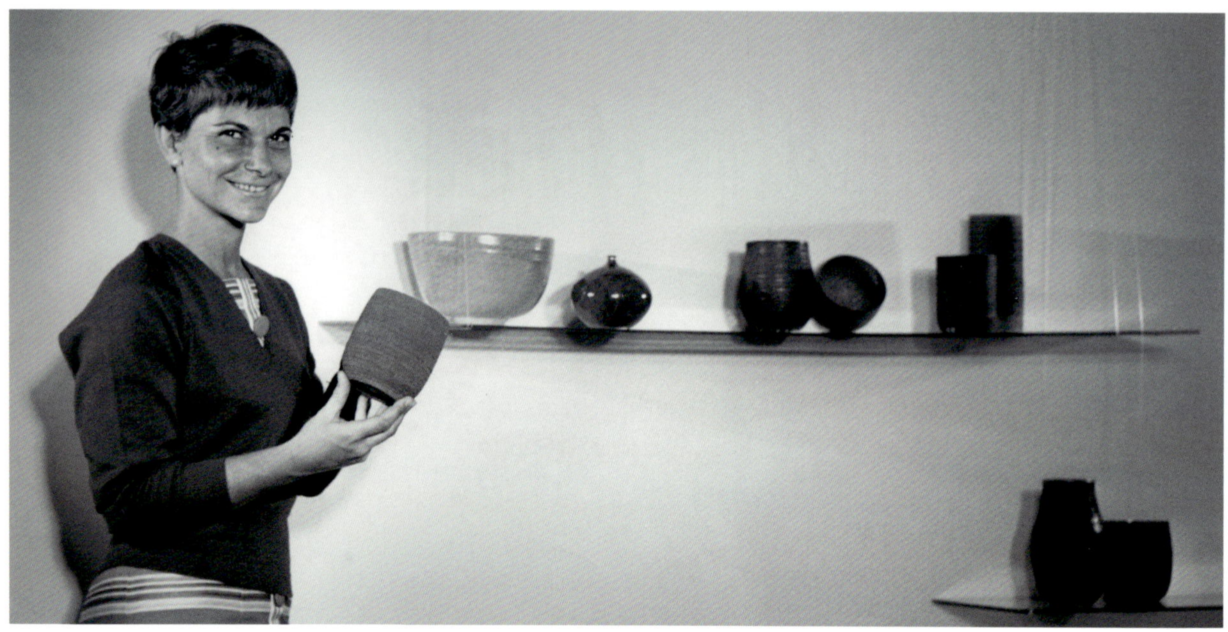

FIG. 6. Tecla Tofano at her solo exhibition *Tecla Tofano: Cerámica* (Ceramics), Museo de Bellas Artes, Caracas, 1961

1960 She participates in the exhibition *Artes del fuego* (Fired Arts) at Sala Mendoza, Caracas.

1961 During a four-year period she produces ceramics at the workshop of the artists Luisa and Gonzalo Palacios. At their workshop, Tofano is interviewed by the Argentinean art critic Clara Diament Sujo [FIG. 5] for the documentary series *El arte en la pantalla* (Art on the Screen) made by the Venezuelan filmmaker and painter Angel Hurtado.

She exhibits thirty-seven ceramics, seven ceramic plates, and fifteen pieces of ceramic and silver jewelry at the Museo de Bellas Artes, Caracas [FIGS. 6–7].

The Third Congress of the Venezuelan Communist Party, influenced by the triumph of the Cuban Revolution, announces its anti-democratic strategy of initiating an armed struggle in order to take control of the government by force.

1962 Tofano is part of the group of ceramists chosen by Miguel Arroyo to participate in the International Exhibition of Contemporary Ceramics held in Prague, Czechoslovakia, and the International Exhibition of Ceramics held in Buenos Aires, Argentina. She is awarded the silver and gold medals, respectively.

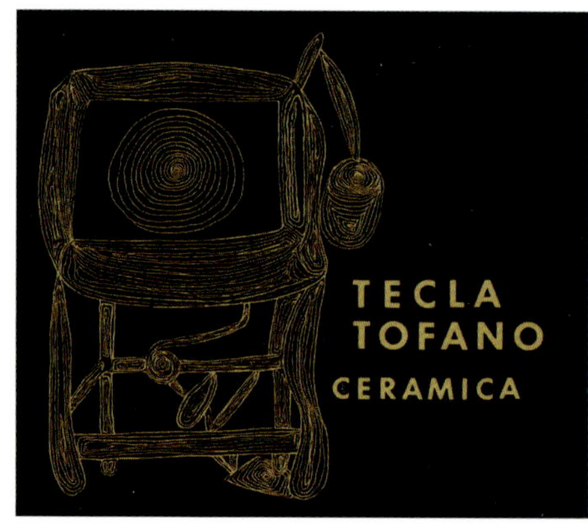

FIG. 7. Cover of the catalogue for *Tecla Tofano: Cerámica*, Museo de Bellas Artes, Caracas, 1961

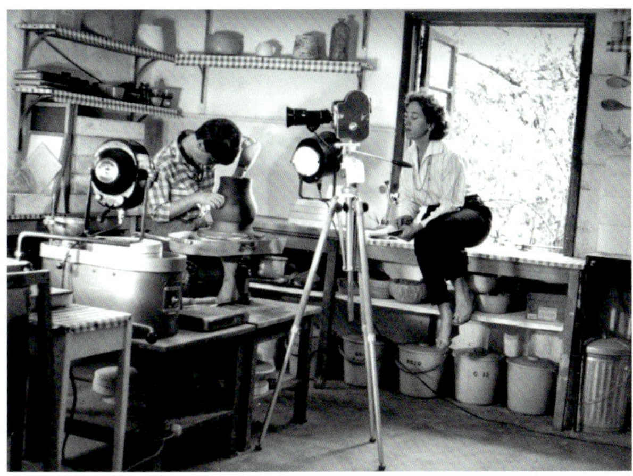

FIG. 5. Clara Diament Sujo interviews Tecla Tofano in her workshop, 1961

Galería El Muro, Caracas, hosts a solo exhibition of her ceramics and silver jewelry [FIG. 8].

She marries the sociologist, writer, and poet Alfredo Chacón.

Having participated in both the attempted coup d'état—called El Carupanazo—in the city of Carúpano and the El Porteñazo uprising in Puerto Cabello, the Venezuelan Communist Party's activities are prohibited and declared illegal. Members of the party continue their activities secretly.

1963 The Museum of Contemporary Crafts (now the Museum of Arts and Design) in New York City includes her work in a group exhibition of Venezuelan ceramists titled *Venezuelan Pottery*.

She exhibits in the 9th International Exhibition of Ceramic Art at the Smithsonian Museum and the Pan-American Union Museum in Washington, DC.

Participates in the Exposición Internacional de Cerámica (International Ceramic Exhibition) at the Teatro Auditórium Casino Central, Mar del Plata, Argentina.

American writer Betty Friedan publishes *The Feminine Mystique*, which is widely credited with laying the groundwork for the second-wave feminism social movement (1968–85) in the United States and other western nations.

Exhibits with sculptor Harry Abend and painter Luisa Palacios in the exhibition *Pintura, cerámica y escultura* (Painting, Ceramics, and Sculpture) at the Museo de Bellas Artes, Caracas.

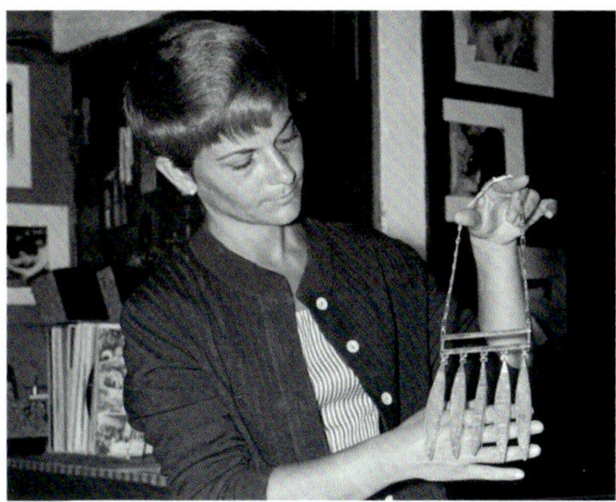

FIG. 8. Tecla Tofano with her jewelry, 1962

1964 Her solo exhibition at the Museo de Bellas Artes, Caracas, includes for the first time drawings and hand-modeled ceramics in addition to thrown vessels [FIG. 9].

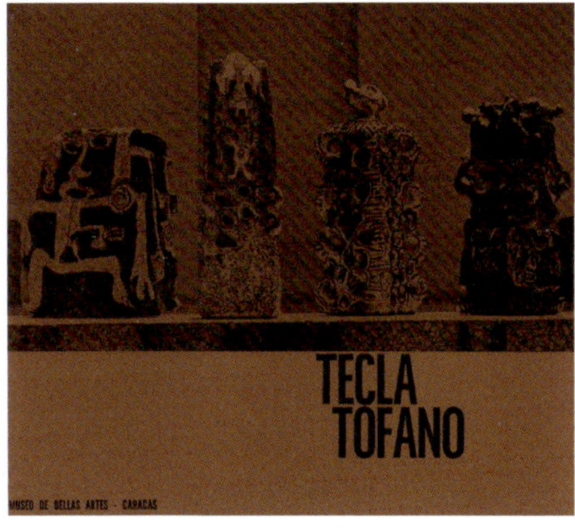

FIG. 9. Cover of the catalogue for *Tecla Tofano: Cerámicas*, Museo de Bellas Artes, Caracas, 1964

Tofano explains her motivations for the inclusion of drawings in this show:

I got rid of my prejudices . . . I only know that the result of my work is dictated by an urgent need to say things, to talk to everyone, to talk about everything and not knowing how to do it. My pieces could have been stories, if I had known how to write; conferences, if I had known how to speak . . . My drawings are spontaneous graphic sketchings, and I thought it was necessary to join them to my pieces, even though individually they have nothing to do with each one of them. They are further explanations of what I do.[5]

Her ceramics are exhibited in the Venezuelan Pavilion at the New York World's Fair.

She gives birth to her second daughter, Claudia Chacón Tofano.

1965 She publishes *¿Quien inventó la silla?* (Who Invented the Chair?), a book of children's stories illustrated with her drawings and dedicated to her son, Daniel [FIG. 10].

Solo exhibition of her drawings at Galería El Pez Dorado, Caracas [FIG. 11].

She is included in a group exhibition at Galería El Techo de la Ballena, Caracas.

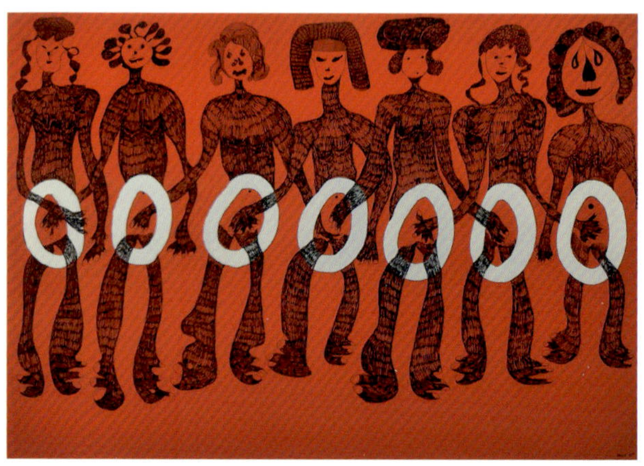

FIG. 14. Tecla Tofano, *Sin título* (Untitled), 1967. Chinese ink and gouache on cardboard; 19⅝ × 23⅝ in. (50 × 60 cm)

1966 Under the auspices of the Fina Gómez Foundation, the Museo de Bellas Artes de Caracas inaugurates *Del Pierre, Hamada, Leach*, an exhibition of great relevance given its influence on the Venezuelan ceramics movement. The exhibition included artworks created by international ceramics masters Francine Del Pierre, Shōji Hamada, and Bernard Leach, in addition to the work of Venezuelan artists, including Seka Severin de Tudja, Reina Herrera,

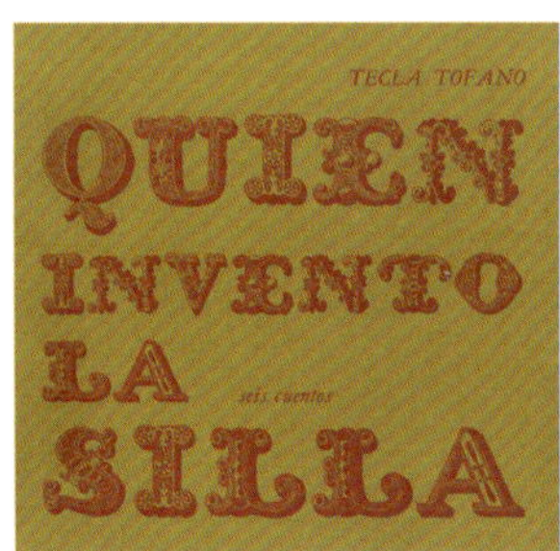

FIG. 10. Cover of Tecla Tofano, *¿Quien inventó la silla?* (Who Invented the Chair?), Editorial Arte, Caracas, 1965

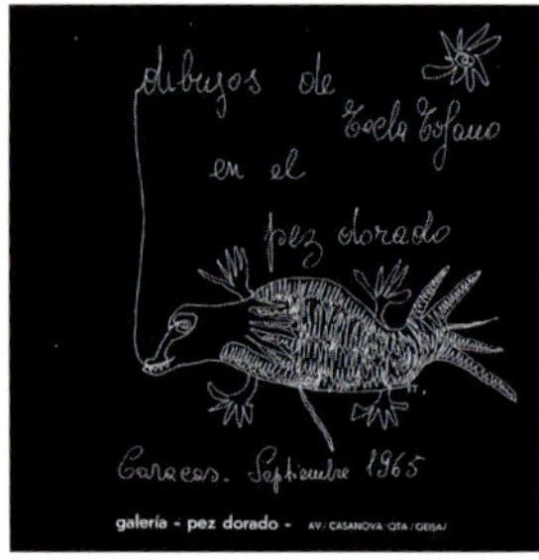

FIG. 11. Cover of the catalogue for *Tecla Tofano: Dibujos* (Drawings), Galería El Pez Dorado, Caracas, 1965

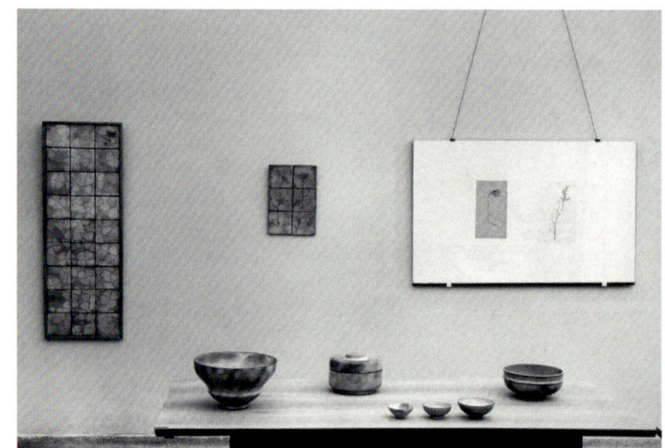

FIG. 12. View of the exhibition *Del Pierre, Hamada, Leach* at Museo de Bellas Artes, Caracas, 1966

and Tecla Tofano. Bernard Leach and Francine Del Pierre travel to Venezuela for the exhibition, organizing workshops, lectures, and demonstrations that contribute decisively to the training of local artists [FIG. 12].

Solo exhibition of her ceramics and drawings at the Museo de Bellas Artes, Caracas.

Graphic designer and painter Gerd Leufert designs Tofano's personal ceramic stamp signature [FIG. 13].

1967 Exhibits twenty-nine drawings and seven gouaches on paper at Galería Polo & Bot, Caracas [FIG. 14].

She participates in the group show *Cerámicas* (Ceramics) at Galería Gamma, Caracas.

Tofano writes the chapter "El hombre y la cerámica" (Man and Ceramics) for Juan Calzadilla's book *El arte en Venezuela* (Art in Venezuela), a compendium of essays on the history, diverse manifestations, and relevant creators of Venezuelan art.[6]

1968 The second-wave feminist movement takes hold in the United States. On September 7, several hundred women demonstrate against the Miss America pageant in Atlantic City, New Jersey, decrying the objectification of women. Issues such as rape, reproductive rights, domestic violence, and workplace safety are given precedence.

She inaugurates her first thematic solo exhibition *Hábitat y habitantes* (Habitat and Inhabitants) at the Museo de Bellas Artes, Caracas. On display are fifty-five hand-modeled pieces and thirty-five wheel-thrown vessels. Art critic Roberto Guevara describes Tofano's work in this exhibition:

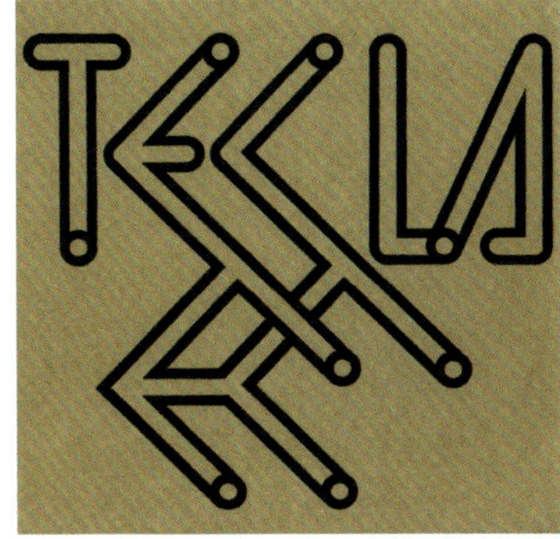

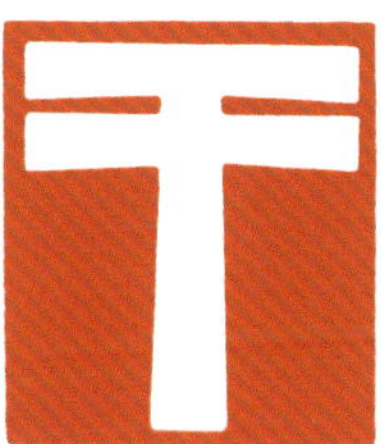

FIG. 15. Cover of the catalogue for *De la silla a la cápsula* (From the Chair to the Capsule), Sala Mendoza, Caracas, 1969

FIG. 13. Tecla Tofano's personal ceramic stamp signature, designed by Gerd Leufert, 1966

Tecla takes out of the earth her "hábitats"; these are the dwellings of men through the times and of the artist's unleashed imagination. Singular towers, full of inscriptions, reliefs, sculptural elements: columns to inhabit the human through signs and forms of a leafy and strong baroque. Nature and the human mingle, projecting each other. It is the living dialogue, so delicately captured by Tofano.[7]

Solo exhibition of drawings at Galería XX2, Caracas.

She participates in the International Exhibition of Ceramics in Istanbul, Turkey.

1969 Solo exhibition *De la silla a la cápsula* (From the Chair to the Capsule), Sala Mendoza, Caracas [FIG. 15]. Regarding the work in her recent exhibition, Tofano explains:

I do not believe in applied arts, minor or major arts. Nor do I believe that I am solving a sculptural problem. The forms are just my way of expressing myself and are felt as such. Design interests me to the extent that it serves me to say what I want to say. If baroque, if convoluted, if unpleasant to the eye,

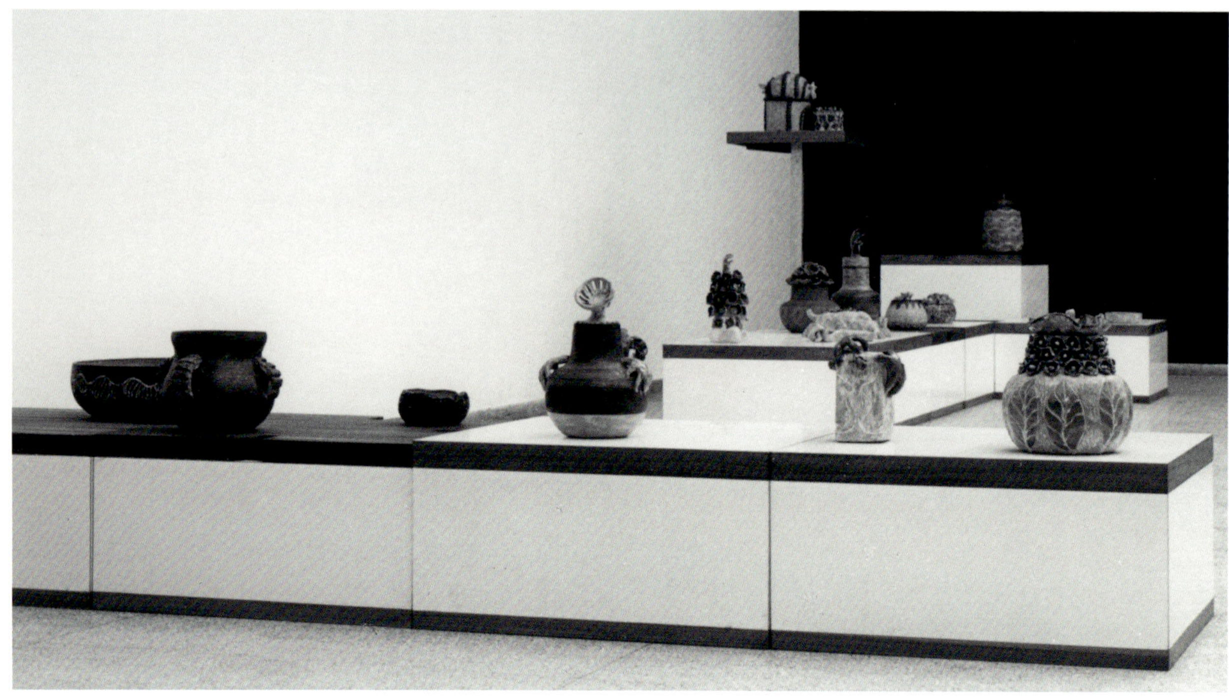

FIG. 17. View of Tecla Tofano's exhibition *Los enlatados (The Canned)* at Museo de Bellas Artes, Caracas, 1970

if shocking in some occasions, it is because what I want to say is not pretty.[8]

Solo exhibition *Recortes* (Clippings) at Museo de Bellas Artes, Caracas [FIG. 16].

1970 Solo exhibition of hand-modeled ceramics *Los enlatados* (The Canned) at Museo de Bellas Artes, Caracas [FIG. 17]. Critic Marta Traba describes the works as "pieces in which people struggle to get out of prison-like dwellings—hands, clawing and gesticulating in the air trying to free themselves from the box, can or prison where they are pitted against each other."[9]

She participates in the group exhibition *Artes del fuego* (Fired Arts), Sala Mendoza, Caracas.

1971 Tofano writes her autobiographical fiction, *Un trozo de historia* (A Piece of History), which is awarded honorable mention in the Concurso de Literatura José Rafael Pocaterra (José Rafael

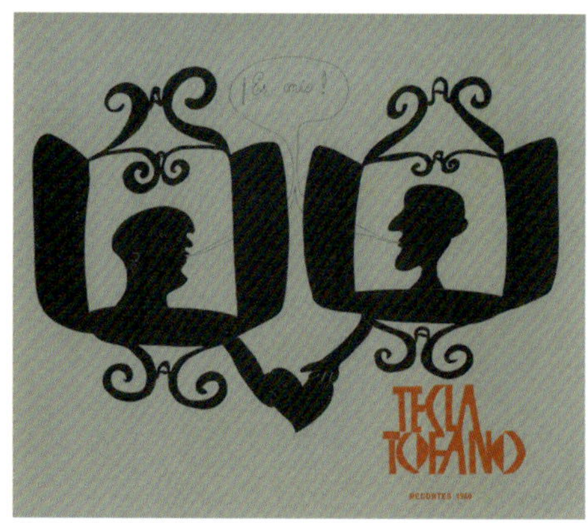

FIG. 16. Cover of the catalogue for *Tecla Tofano: Recortes* (Clippings), Museo de Bellas Artes, Caracas, 1969

Pocaterra Literature Contest) at the Ateneo
de Valencia, Venezuela.

She receives an honorary diploma in a competition
on theater writing for children organized by the
Consejo Venezolano del Niño, Caracas.

Her solo exhibition *La cama y sus posibilidades*
(The Bed and Its Possibilities) at Galería El Círculo
de Piedra and Galería Viva México in Caracas,
features thirty hand-modeled pieces and
seventeen drawings [FIG. 18].

The critic Marta Traba elaborates on this exhibition:

*"La cama y sus posibilidades" is undoubtedly Tofano's
statement of principles concerning her* ars politica. *She
returns time and again to her constant themes, using
them repeatedly as true purveyors of meaning. One
of her themes, to teach from the very beginning, was
already present in the "Hábitat y habitantes" series
that began in the cave and the "De la silla a la cápsula"
series. That naïve, pedagogical, recurring desire is
driven by the same all-encompassing eagerness to say
"everything," to review the process from the very start
and tell it all over again. Which is, incidentally, one of*

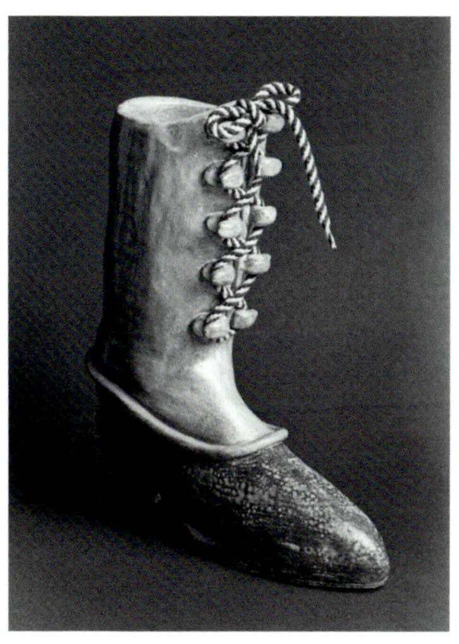

FIG. 19. Tecla Tofano, *Mi madre fue joven*
(My Mother Was Young), from the
series *Los accesorios* (The Accessories),
1971. Glazed ceramic; 8¼ × 6 × 4 in.
(21 × 15 × 10 cm)

*the traits of children's art and primitive art. With the
difference that Tecla—unlike children and primitive
people—presents a view of the world that is fueled
by a critical spirit. She is not just proffering a series of
explorations or perspectives; her discourses condemn and
seek to correct the situations they encounter.*[10]

Tofano presents her exhibition *Los accesorios*
(The Accessories) at Galería Banap, Caracas [FIG. 19].
It consists of forty-four hand-modeled pieces and
eight drawings. Critic Marta Traba highlights its
main theme:

*"The Accessories", more so than "The Bed and its
Possibilities", attacks the consumer society and its
fashions, whims, atrocities, and erosion.*[11]

Her work is part of the *Salón de artes del fuego* (Fired
Arts Salon) in Valencia and the exhibition *Artes del
fuego* (Fired Arts) at Sala Mendoza, Caracas.

She joins Movimiento al Socialismo (MAS)
—a new political party grounded in democratic

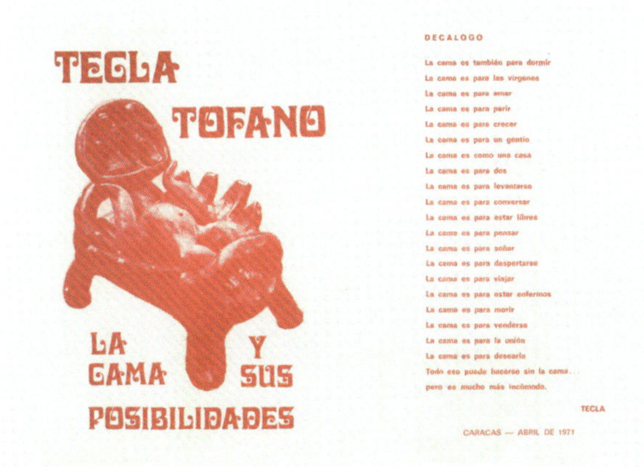

FIG. 18. Cover of the catalogue for *Tecla Tofano: La cama y sus
posibilidades* (The Bed and Its Possibilities), Galería Viva México,
Caracas, 1971

socialist ideology—as a militant and activist. MAS was founded by a group of leaders from the ranks of the Venezuelan Communist Party.

1972 She gives birth to her third daughter, Carla Chacón Tofano.

Participates in the International Exhibition of Ceramics organized by the Victoria and Albert Museum, London, UK.

She creates the suite of forty-four drawings made in pencil on paper titled *Evas al desnudo* (Naked Eves), [FIG. 20] whose powerful representations of archetypal scenarios involving women underscores Tofano's militant and experiential feminist discourse.

Solo exhibition *Tecla de remate* at Galería Aztlan, Caracas.

Shows her work at the *Artes del fuego* (Fired Arts), Sala Mendoza, Caracas.

A group of women led by Tofano, Argelia Laya, Josefina Acevedo, Franca Donda, and Josefina

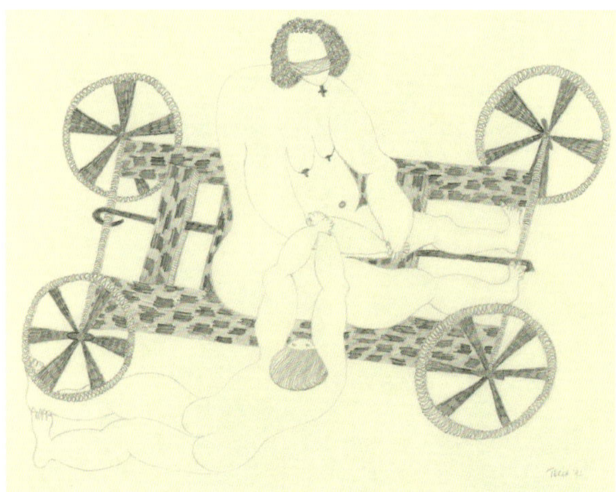

FIG. 20. Tecla Tofano, *Hacia la utopía* (Toward Utopia), from the suite *Evas al desnudo* (Naked Eves), 1972. Pencil on paper; 8¼ × 10⅝ in. (21.5 × 27 cm)

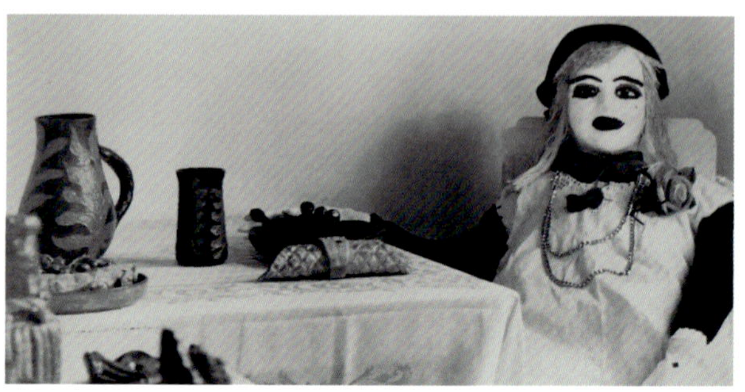

FIG. 21. View of the exhibition *Lo que comen los que comen* (What Those Who Eat Eat), Galería Viva México, Caracas, 1973

Jordán, among others, creates the feminist collective Mujeres Socialistas del MAS to promote women's inclusion and effective participation in Venezuela's political life.

1973 Solo exhibition *Lo que comen los que comen* (What Those Who Eat Eat) at Galería Viva México, Caracas [FIG. 21]. Tofano stages an installation of a large banquet that includes forty-seven hand-modeled ceramics and twelve collages. Critic Marta Traba describes the installation:

The bold confrontation of "Lo que comen los que comen" launches an attack, an unvarnished condemnation of the kinds of orgiastic feasts associated with the elite who reap the benefits of consumer society. She stages a grotesque scene involving a table set with her ceramic banquet surrounded by rag-doll dinner guests sitting stiffly, their faces heavily made up, reveling in the bacchanalian pleasures of the sort of gastronomic excesses pictured in magazines.[12]

Tofano debuts *Esa munda macha*, a solo exhibition whose theme confronts the scaffolding on which a patriarchal society is built [FIG. 22]. The exhibition's thirty hand-modeled ceramic pieces contain phallic elements that explore the spheres of influence and conditioning of a patriarchal worldview.

She exhibits twelve of her ceramics with works by Carlos Raúl Villanueva, Gego, and Gerd Leufert, among others, in the collective exhibition of professors and graduates *20 años de la Facultad de Arquitectura de la UCV* (20 Years of the UCV's Faculty of Architecture), UCV, Caracas.

1974 Her solo exhibition *30 pecados vitales* (30 Vital Sins) at Galería Sala Ocre, Caracas features twelve drawings and thirty hand-modeled ceramics. Within each of these outstanding pieces, Tofano crafts the word pertinent to its corresponding vital sin: *Decir* (To Say) [FIG. 23], *Coito* (Coitus), *Defecar* (To Defecate), *Vejez* (Old Age).

She presents her book *Yo misma me presento* (I Introduce Myself) [FIG. 24], Tofano's vision concerning the female experience. In the introduction to the book, she expresses the impetus for writing this autobiographical fiction:

So almost suddenly it seemed important to me to give my life experiences, under certain aspects and from myself as a woman. I wanted to tell you all those things even in a bad state, for many, because I want to push others to say without waiting for death or infinity to come to know everything, to correct us, to prepare us while we have not had the necessary and important opportunities until today, perhaps until tomorrow and beyond.[13]

She participates in *Artes del Fuego* (Fired Arts), Sala Mendoza, Caracas.

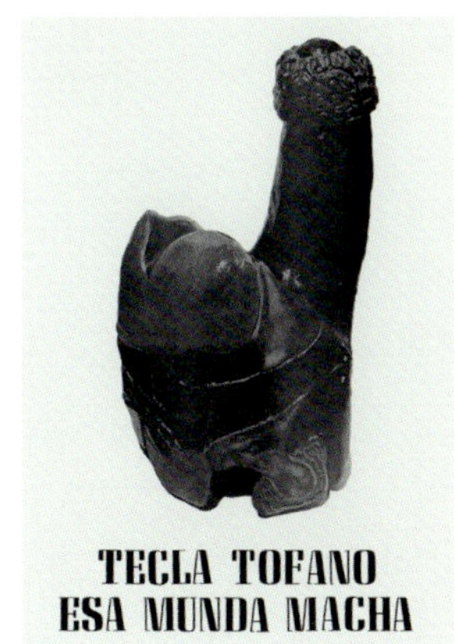

FIG. 22. Cover of the catalogue for *Tecla Tofano: Esa munda macha*, Galería Viva México, Caracas, 1973

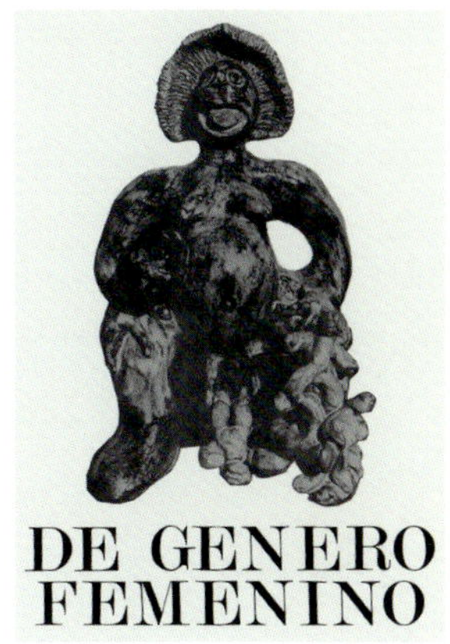

FIG. 25. Cover of the catalogue for *De género femenino* (Of the Female Gender), Galería Viva México, Caracas, 1975

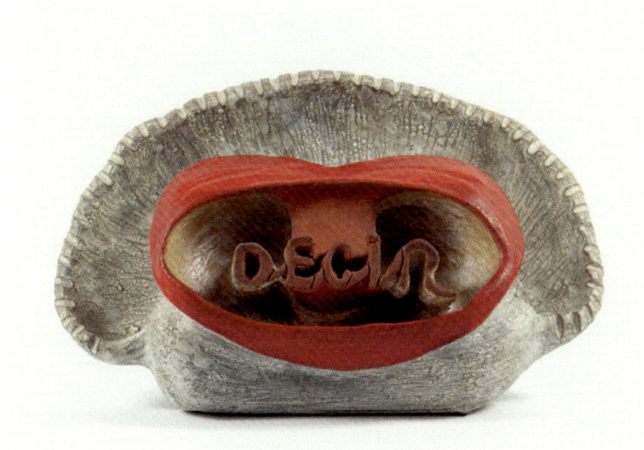

FIG. 23. Tecla Tofano, *Decir* (To Say), from her series *30 pecados vitales* (30 Vital Sins), 1974. Glazed ceramic; 6 ¼ × 10 ¼ × 6 ¼ in. (16 × 26 × 16cm)

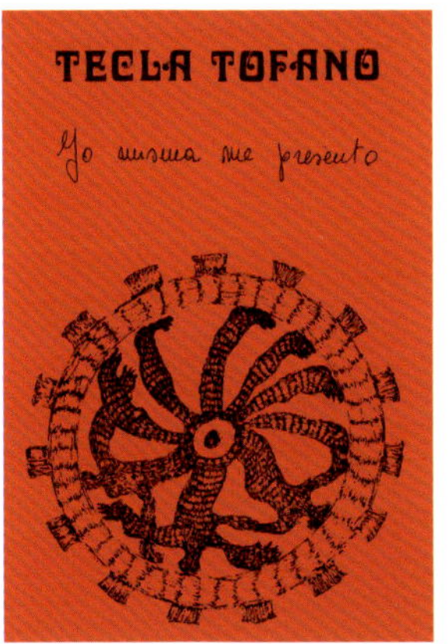

FIG. 24. Cover of Tecla Tofano, *Yo misma me presento* (I Introduce Myself), Editorial La Avispa, Caracas, 1974

1975 Her solo exhibition entitled *De género femenino* (Of the Female Gender), featuring thirty-two hand-modeled ceramics whose discourse is based on the female body, debuts at Galería Viva México, Caracas [FIG.25]. In this series, Tofano points out stigmas faced by women in a patriarchal society.

El libro y su evasión (The Book and Its Evasion), a solo show with seventeen hand-modeled ceramics and their respective drawings, is held at Galería Cruz del Sur, Caracas [FIG.26].

She launches her book *Ni con el pétalo de una rosa* (Not Even with a Rose Petal), a compilation of articles published in the weekly magazine *Punto*, Caracas.

Tofano is included in the book *El artista en su taller* (The Artist in His Studio), wherein the historian, writer, artist, and critic Juan Calzadilla documents his visit to the workshop of twenty-five Venezuelan artists whom he considers of great relevance.[14]

1976 Participates in *Artes del Fuego* (Fired Arts), Sala Mendoza, Caracas.

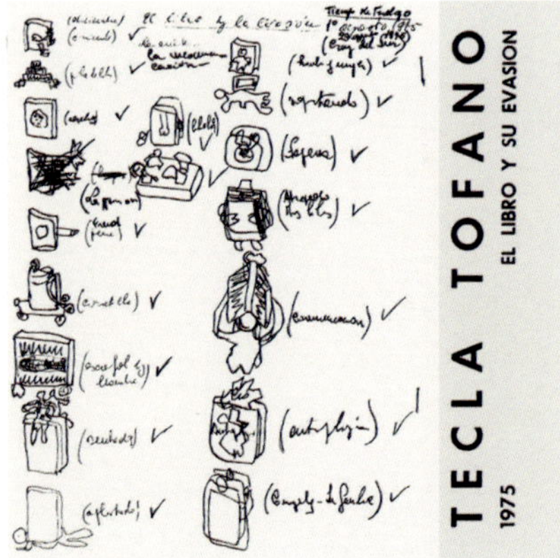

FIG.26. Cover of the catalogue for *Tecla Tofano: El libro y su evasión* (The Book and Its Evasion), Galería Cruz del Sur, Caracas, 1975

1977 She is featured in the exhibition *Taller de cerámica* (Ceramic Workshop) at Museo de Arte Contemporáneo de Caracas Sofía Ímber, Caracas.

Solo exhibition *Las señoras* (Ladies) at Galería CONAC, Caracas [FIGS. 27–28]. The artist elaborates on the crude reality of the married woman's behavior as exemplified in thirty ceramic heads. Tofano explores topics ranging from fierce self-criticism from a feminine perspective to the conventional structure and legal framework in which women themselves contribute to their oppressive circumstances in order to "fit" into a social status.

Tofano is included in *Escultura/Escultores* (Sculpture/Sculptors), a book on sculpture in Venezuela published by Juan Calzadilla and Pedro Briceño.[15]

Ella, él . . . ellos (She, He . . . They) solo exhibition at Galería de Arte Nacional, Caracas in which Tecla Tofano announces her retirement as a ceramist. In the catalogue, the artist elaborates by saying:

My own conceptual and technical limitations, in the need for denunciation and the limiting expressive medium itself, are perhaps the causes of my possible retirement. So, here I present, divided yet united: SHE, HE and this new imaginary being, symbol at last of a possible symbiosis of essential values of man and woman, without discrimination and limitation.[16]

She cofounds the Grupo Feminista Miércoles (Feminist Group Miércoles) with Giovanna Mérola, Josefina Acevedo, Ambretta Marrossu, and Franca Donda, among others.

1978 Her work is included in the book *La tierra doctorada* (The Cultured Earth) by Rafael Pineda, a writer and researcher whose work considers various topics on the history of handicrafts and pre-Columbian, modern, and popular ceramics in Venezuela.[17]

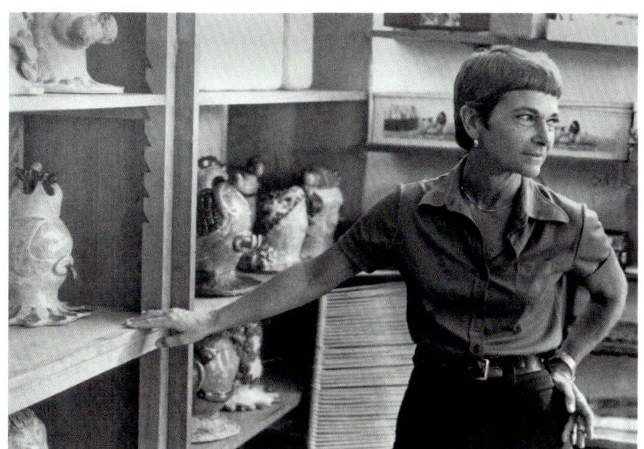

FIG. 27. Tecla Tofano in her studio, 1977

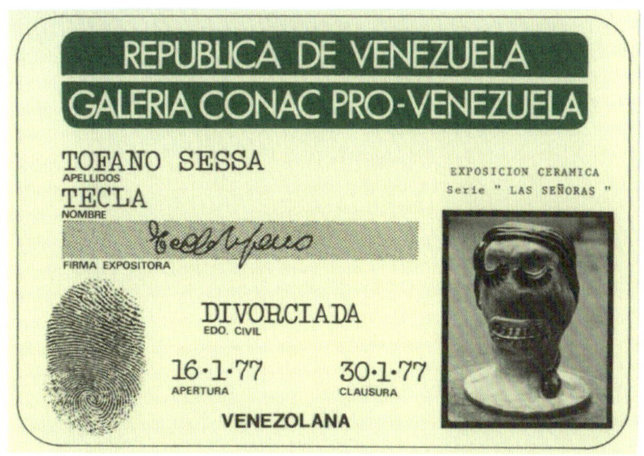

FIG. 28. Cover of the catalogue for *Tecla Tofano: Las señoras* (Ladies), Galería CONAC, Caracas, 1977

Roberto Guevara, an art critic and promoter of Latin American ceramics, publishes *Las manos en el barro* (Hands in the Clay), a book reviewing the work of twenty-three Venezuelan ceramists, including Tofano.[18]

1980 Tofano contributes her writing regularly to the newspaper *El Nacional* in Caracas and continues until 1993.

1982 After years of struggle, Venezuelan women achieve civil code reform that establishes their legal equality with men in marriage.

1987 Solo exhibition *Dibujos y collages* (Drawings and Collages), Galería Espacios Cálidos, Ateneo de Caracas. In the catalogue introduction, Tofano discusses this show that came after her retirement as a ceramist:

It has been ten years since I last exhibited. I retired from making ceramics, not from other expressions. I feel like a sculptor. I could never be one in practice for reasons that are no longer relevant. In my spare time, which is not much, I draw without knowing how to do it. So I simply say that I am self-taught;

I don't know how to draw according to established patterns. I have fun, and above all, I release my emotions. I can't help it. My interest is to communicate, even in this primitive form. And I dedicate it all to those women among whom we understand that we love each other, even if it costs us a lot, because of mistakes inherent to the very fact of being a woman.[19]

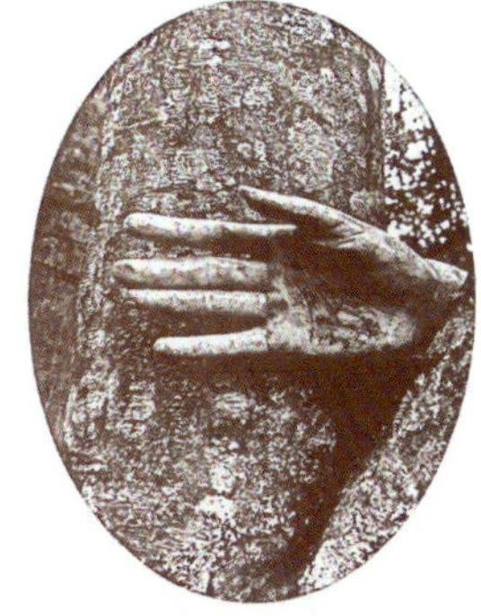

FIG. 29. Cover of *Epílogos* (Epilogues), Caracas, 1987

She publishes her book of poetry *Epílogos* (Epilogues) [FIG. 29].[20]

1989 Her solo exhibition of twenty-three drawings in crayon, *El Tarot—Arcano Mayor, 22 + 0* (The Tarot—Major Arcana, 22 + 0), debuts at Galería Viva México, Caracas.

1992 She collaborates in the foundation of Centro de Estudios de la Mujer (Center for Women's Studies) at UCV.

1993 She is awarded with the José María Vargas Medal, UCV.

1995 Tecla Tofano dies on October 20 at the age of 68.

1996 UCV inaugurates the Centro de Documentación Tecla Tofano (Tecla Tofano Documentation Center) in recognition of her social commitment to the cause of women's rights and her creation of important Venezuelan feminist groups.

1999 Researcher and art critic Nelly Barbieri publishes *El movimiento cerámico en Venezuela* (The Ceramics Movement in Venezuela), the only publication to date that systematically studies the origin, evolution, and development of the history of modern Venezuelan ceramics[21].

2015 Her work is included in the exhibition *Moderno: Design for living in Brazil, Mexico and Venezuela, 1940–1978*, Americas Society, New York.

2017 She is featured in the exhibition *Radical Women: Latin American Art, 1960–1985* organized by the Hammer Museum, Los Angeles, California.

2018 Tofano's ceramics are part of *Contesting Modernity: Informalism in Venezuela, 1955–1975* at the Museum of Fine Arts, Houston, Texas.

2022 Tofano's works are selected by curator Cecilia Alemani to be part of the 59th International Art Exhibition La Biennale di Venezia—*Il latte dei sogni* (Venice Biennale—The Milk of Dreams) in Venice, Italy [FIG. 30].

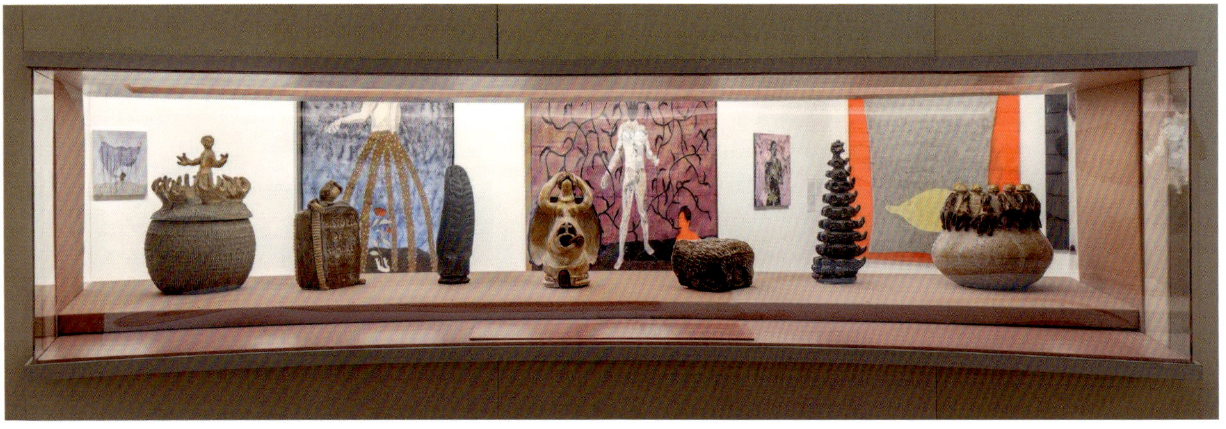

FIG. 30. View of Tecla Tofano's works at the 59th International Art Exhibition La Biennale di Venezia —*Il latte dei sogni* (Venice Biennale—The Milk of Dreams), 2022

NOTES

1. Tecla Tofano interviewed by José Francisco Castillo, December 16, 1992, Tecla Tofano folder, Centro de Información y Documentacion Nacional de las Artes Plasticas, Galería de Arte Nacional, Caracas. Unless otherwise noted, all translations are my own.

2. Tecla Tofano, "Ceramista Venezolana," *Punto* (September 1963).

3. Miguel Arroyo, "Cristina Merchan y Tecla Tofano, dos ceramistas," *Integral*, No. 9 (November 1957), unpaginated.

4. Miguel Arroyo, introduction to *Tecla Tofano, cerámica*, exh. cat. (Caracas: Museo de Bellas Artes, 1959).

5. Tecla Tofano, introduction to *Tecla Tofano, exposición de cerámica*, exh. cat. (Caracas: Museo de Bellas Artes, 1964).

6. Juan Calzadilla, *El arte en Venezuela* (Caracas: Ediciones Círculo Musical, 1967), 145–49.

7. Roberto Guevara, *Ver todos los días* (Caracas: Monte Ávila Editores, 1981), 162–63.

8. Tecla Tofano, introduction to *De la silla a la cápsula*, exh. cat. (Caracas, Sala de Exposiciones Fundación Eugenio Mendoza: 1969).

9. Marta Traba, "Tecla Tofano: Ars Politica," *El Nacional*, March 11, 1973. Translation by Anthony Beckwith.

10. Traba, "Tecla Tofano."

11. Traba, "Tecla Tofano."

12. Traba, "Tecla Tofano."

13. Tecla Tofano, *Yo misma me presento* (Caracas, Editorial la Avispa, 1974), back cover.

14. Juan Calzadilla, *El artista en su taller* (Caracas: Editorial La Huella, 1975), 161–68.

15. Juan Calzadilla and Pedro Briceño, *Escultura/ Escultores, Un libro sobre la escultura en Venezuela* (Caracas: Editorial La Huella, 1977), 212, 229–30.

16. Tecla Tofano, introduction to *Ella, él . . . ellos*, exh. cat. (Caracas: Galería de Arte Nacional, 1978).

17. Rafael Pineda, *La tierra doctorada* (Caracas: Ernesto Armitano Editor, 1978), 325–37, 371, 537.

18. Roberto Guevara, *Las manos en el barro* (Caracas: Editorial La Huella, 1978), 142–47.

19. Tecla Tofano, introduction to *Dibujos*, exh. cat. (Caracas: Los Espacios Cálidos, 1987), 2.

20. Tecla Tofano, *Epílogos* (Caracas: Ediciones La Draga y el Dragón, 1987).

21. Nelly Barbieri, *El movimiento cerámico en Venezuela* (Caracas: Consejo Nacional de Cultura (CONAC), 1999), 68–69.

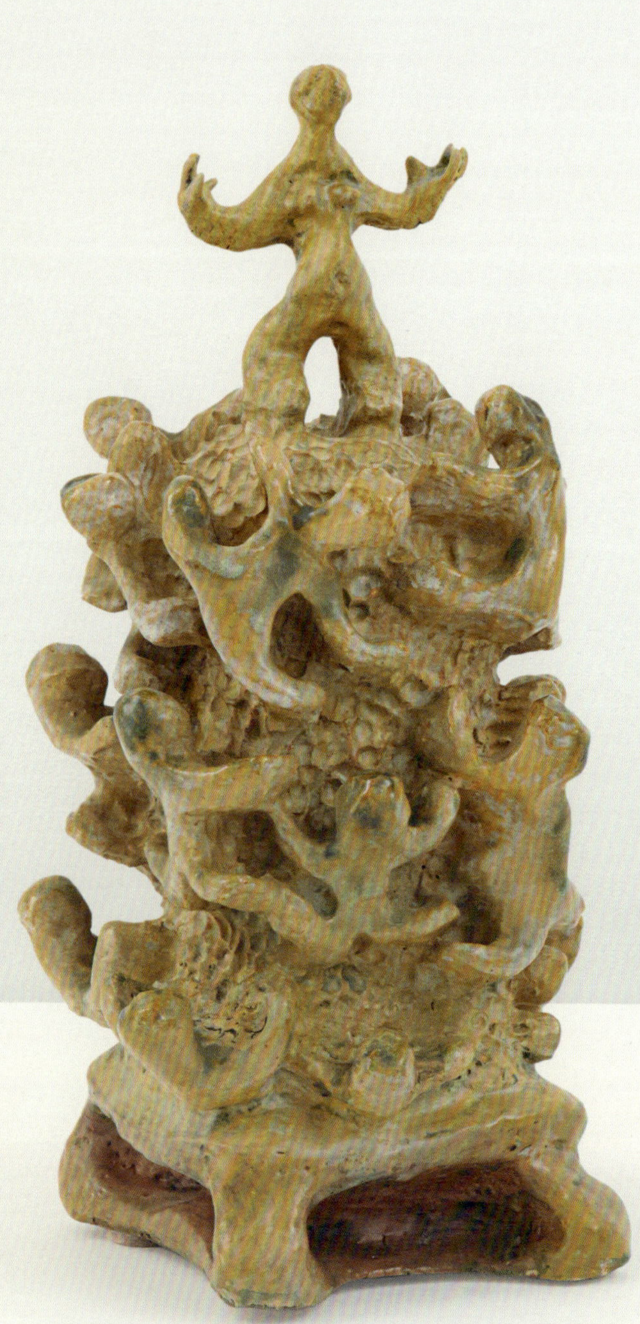

LIST OF WORKS

Sin título (Untitled),
small globular vase, 1959
Ceramic
3½ × 5 × 5 in. (9 × 12.5 × 12.5 cm)
P. 32

Sin título (Untitled),
tall vase, 1959
Ceramic
8½ × 5½ × 5½ in. (22 × 14.5 × 14.5 cm)
P. 33

Sin título (Untitled),
tall cylindrical vase, 1961
Glazed ceramic
10 × 3½ × 3½ in. (25.4 × 8.9 × 8.9 cm)
P. 34

Sin título (Untitled),
small tower, 1964
Glazed ceramic
6¼ × 2¼ × 2¼ in. (15.9 × 5.7 × 5.7 cm)
P. 62

NOTES:
All dimensions are listed
as height × width × depth
or diameter.

All works are courtesy
of private collections.

Sin título (Untitled),
vase with drippage, 1964
Glazed ceramic
9 ½ × 7 × 7 in. (24.1 × 17.8 × 17.8 cm)
P. 35

Sin título (Untitled),
ashtray, 1965
Glazed ceramic
2 ½ × 4 × 4 in. (6.3 × 10.2 × 10.2 cm)
P. 34

Lengua (Tongue), 1966
Glazed ceramic
8 ¾ × 3 ½ × 3 in. (22.2 × 8.9 × 7.6 cm)
P. 54

Sin título (Untitled), 1966
Glazed ceramic
11 × 4 ½ × 4 ½ in. (27.9 × 11.4 × 11.4 cm)
PP. 40–41

Lengua tótem
(Totem Tongue), 1966
Glazed ceramic
12 ½ × 4 × 3 in. (31.8 × 10.2 × 7.6 cm)
PP. 38–39

Sin título (Untitled),
small floral vase, 1967
Glazed ceramic
7 ½ × 3 ½ × 3 ½ in. (19.1 × 8.9 × 8.9 cm)
PP. 58–59

Hábitat dragón
(Habitat Dragon), 1967
From the series *Hábitat y habitantes*
(Habitats and Inhabitants)
Glazed ceramic
15 × 6 × 5 in. (38.1 × 15.2 × 12.7 cm)
PP. 44–45

Bastión (Bastion), 1967
From the series *Hábitat y habitantes*
(Habitats and Inhabitants)
Glazed ceramic
14 × 6 × 6 in.
(35.6 × 15.2 × 15.2 cm)
P. 47

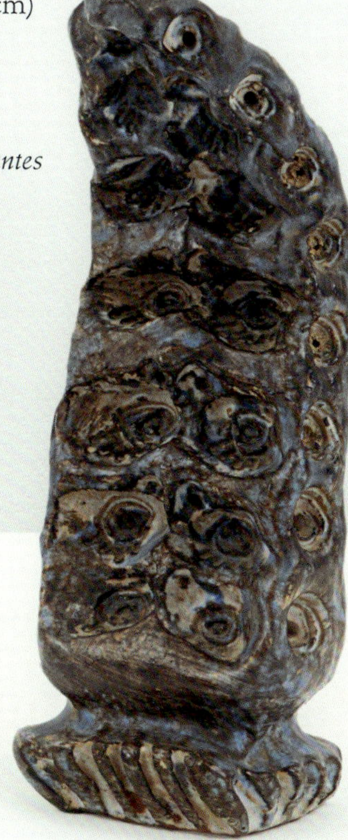

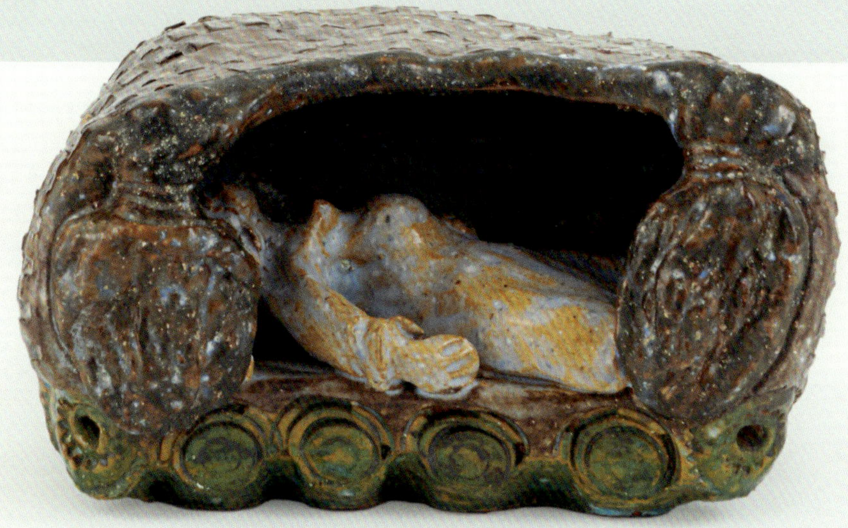

Vasija con personaje
(Vessel with Personage), 1969
From the series *Los enlatados* (The Canned)
Glazed ceramic
15 ½ × 8 × 8 in. (39.4 × 20.3 × 20.3 cm)
PP. 42–43

Monumento a la rueda
(Wheel Monument), 1969
From the series *De la silla a la cápsula*
(From the Chair to the Capsule)
Glazed ceramic
14 ¾ × 12 ½ × ¾ in. (37.5 × 31.5 × 2 cm)
P. 48

Sin título (Untitled),
bulbous vase, 1969
Glazed ceramic
8 × 8 × 8 in. (20.5 × 20.5 × 20.5 cm)
P. 36

Sin título (Untitled), 1970
From the series *Los enlatados* (The Canned)
Glazed ceramic
8 ½ × 7 ½ × 6 ¼ in. (22 × 19 × 16 cm)
P. 51

Baldaquín (Canopy Bed), 1971
From the series *La cama y sus posibilidades*
(The Bed and Its Possibilities)
Glazed ceramic
9 × 6 × 9 in. (23 × 15 × 23 cm)
P. 66

Wagon-Lit, 1971
From the series *La cama y sus posibilidades*
(The Bed and Its Possibilities)
Glazed ceramic
4 ½ × 8 × 5 ½ (11.4 × 20.3 × 14 cm)
P. 49

Cuando me levanto (When I Wake Up), 1971
From the series *Los accesorios* (The Accessories)
Glazed ceramic
4 ½ × 3 × 8 in. (11.4 × 7.6 × 20.3 cm)
P. 62

Cinturón con cartera (Belt with Purse), 1971
From the series *Los accesorios* (The Accessories)
Glazed ceramic
2 ½ × 6 ½ × 7 in. (6.3 × 16.5 x 17.8 cm)
P. 46

Sin título (Untitled), lidded vessel, 1972
Glazed ceramic
13 × 8 ½ × 8 ½ in. (33.5 × 22 × 22 cm)
P. 50

Sin título (Untitled), bowl with sgraffito, 1972
Glazed ceramic
4 ½ × 10 ½ × 10 ½ in. (11 × 27 × 27 cm)
P. 37

Sin título (Untitled), lidded bottle, 1972
Glazed ceramic
13 ¾ × 8 ½ × 8 ½ in. (35 × 22 × 22 cm)
P. 57

Bacalao al limón
(Cod with Lemon), 1973
From the series *Lo que comen los que comen*
(What Those Who Eat Eat)
Glazed ceramic
13 ½ × 9 × 3 ½ in. (34.3 × 22.9 × 8.9 cm)
PP. 52–53

Solidaridad (Solidarity), 1973
From the series *Esa Munda Macha*
Glazed ceramic
10 × 8 ¼ × 6 ¾ in. (25.5 × 21 × 17 cm)
P. 60

Y poblaron al mundo
(And They Populated the World), 1973
From the series *Esa Munda Macha*
Glazed ceramic
8 ½ × 10 × 10 in. (22 × 25.5 × 25.5 cm)
P. 61

Vejez (Old Age), 1974
From the series *30 pecados vitales* (30 Vital Sins)
Glazed ceramic
8 ¼ × 5 ½ × 5 ½ in. (21 × 14 × 14 cm)
P. 63

Sin título (Untitled), 1973
Glazed ceramic, wood base
4 ½ × 4 ¾ × 4 ¾ in. (11.4 × 12.1 × 12.1 cm)
P. 56

Freud, sexología (Freud, Sexology), 1975
From the series *El libro y su evasión*
(The Book and Its Evasion)
Glazed ceramic
6 ½ × 7 ¼ × 5 ½ in. (16.5 × 18.4 × 14 cm)
PP. 64–65

Comunicación
(Communication), 1975
From the series *El libro y su evasión*
(The Book and Its Evasion)
Glazed ceramic
11 ½ × 9 ½ × 7 ½ in. (29 × 24 × 19 cm)
P. 55

La mujer en la historia
(Women in History), 1975
From the series *De género femenino*
(Of the Female Gender)
Glazed ceramic
10 ½ × 7 × 5 in. (26.7 × 17.8 × 12.7 cm)
P. 67

DRAWINGS

All exhibited works are from the suite of
drawings *Evas al desnudo* (Naked Eves) from
1972. All works were created with pencil
on paper and have vertical proportions
of 10⅝ × 8½ in (27 × 21.5 cm), except
as indicated below with an asterisk (*).
These asterisked drawings have horizontal
proportions of 8½ × 10⅝ in. (21.5 × 27 cm).

Amarrada pero frutal (Tied but Fruity) P. 12
Así empezó todo (Thus It All Began) P. 79
Como un Buda (Like a Buddha) P. 76
¡Con el zapato no! (Not with the Shoe!) [UNILLUSTRATED]
¡Coño! (Cunt!) P. 71
El arranque (The Outset)* [UNILLUSTRATED]
Femineidad (Femininity) P. 84
Hacia la utopía (Toward Utopia)* P. 101
La dulce espera (The Sweet Wait) P. 74
La empollada (The Hatching) P. 78
La siguen (They Follow Her) P. 72
Los reproduce (She Reproduces Them) P. 82
Mariposeando (Butterflying) P. 81
Más que unidas, entrelazadas (More Intertwined
than Joined) P. 70
Parirás (You'll Deliver) P. 75
Por aquí no! (Not Here!) P. 83
¿Reina yo? (Me, A Queen?) P. 80
Se le encarama (She Climbs on Him)* [UNILLUSTRATED]
Seductora (Seducer) P. 19
Sola (Alone)* [UNILLUSTRATED]
Tras el abanico (Behind the Fan) P. 73
Tras el biombo (Behind the Screen) P. 77

Tecla Tofano in her workshop, 1961

Tecla Tofano in her workshop, 1968

Installation view, from left to right: *Lengua tótem* (Totem Tongue), 1966; *Freud, sexología* (Freud, Sexology), 1975; *Sin título* (Untitled), 1966; *Cinturón con cartera* (Belt with Purse), 1971

Installation view, from left to right: *Sin título* (Untitled), 1967; *La mujer en la historia* (Women in History), 1975; *Hábitat dragón* (Habitat Dragon), 1967; *Cuando me levanto* (When I Wake Up), 1971

Tecla Tofano in her studio, 1968

Installation view, from left to right: *Bastión* (Bastion), 1967; *Wagon-Lit*, 1971; *Lengua* (Tongue), 1966

Tecla Tofano in her studio, 1977

CREDITS

SELECTED BIBLIOGRAPHY

ALEMANI, Cecilia. *La Biennale di Venezia. 59a esposizione internazionale d'arte: il latte dei sogni.* Venice: La Biennale di Venezia, 2022.

BARBIERI, Nelly. *El movimiento cerámico en Venezuela.* Caracas: Consejo Nacional de Cultura (CONAC), 1999.

CALZADILLA, Juan. *El artista en su taller.* Caracas: Editorial La Huella, 1975.

—. *El arte en Venezuela.* Caracas: Ediciones Círculo Musical, 1967

FAJARDO-HILL, Cecilia, Andrea Giunta, and Marcela Guerrero. *Radical Women: Latin American Art, 1960–1985.* Los Angeles: Armand Hammer Museum of Art and Cultural Center, 2017.

FARÍAS, Luis Felipe, Mary Martínez Torrealba, and Patricia Velasco. *I-conos, cerámica emblemática venezolana.* Caracas: Fundación Sala Mendoza, 2017.

GUEVARA, Ernesto J., Tahía Rivero, and Félix Suazo. *Cerámica venezolana 1955–2008, Colección Mercantil.* Caracas: Maria Leis, Monsanto Servicios de Arte, 2016.

GUEVARA, Roberto. *Las manos en el barro.* Caracas: Editorial La Huella, 1978.

—. *Ver todos los días.* Caracas: Monte Ávila Editores, 1981.

NIÑO, Esmeralda, and Alejandro Salas, eds. *Diccionario biográfico de las artes visuales en Venezuela.* Caracas: Galería de Arte Nacional, 2005.

PINEDA, Rafael. *La tierra doctorada.* Caracas: Ernesto Armitano Editor, 1978.

RAMÍREZ, Mari Carmen, Maria Gaztambide, Josefina Manrique, Gabriela Rangel, and Tahía Rivero. *Contesting Modernity: Informalism in Venezuela, 1955–1975.* New Haven: Yale University Press, 2018.

RANGEL, Gabriela, and Jorge Rivas Pérez. *Moderno: Design for Living in Brazil, Mexico, and Venezuela, 1940–1978.* New York: Americas Society, 2015.

TOFANO, Tecla. *Epílogos.* Caracas: Ediciones La Draga y el Dragón, 1987.

—. *Ni con el pétalo de una rosa.* Caracas: Publisher, 1975*

—. *¿Quien invento la silla?* Caracas: Editorial Arte, 1965.

—. *Yo misma me presento.* Caracas: Editorial La Avispa, 1973.

TRABA, Marta. *Mirar en Caracas.* Caracas: Monte Avila Editores, 1974.

ary # ACKNOWLEDGMENTS

The editors of this catalogue want to acknowledge the incommensurable assitance of the following people and institutions:

The lenders of the exhibition

Beverly Adams
Giuliana Alvarez
Archivo Fotografía Urbana, Caracas
Sagrario Berti
Amalia Caputo
Davide Carbone
Centro de Información y Documentación Nacional de las Artes Plásticas at Galería de Arte Nacional, Caracas
Daniel Córdova Zerpa
Lucia Córdova Zerpa
Gioconda Espina
Fundación Museos Nacionales
Paolo Gasparini
Marina Gasparini Lagrange
Estate of Sarita Guardia de Mendoza
Enrique Hernández de Jesús

International Center for the Arts of the Americas/ Museum of Fine Arts Houston, Texas
Angelina Jaffe Carbonell
James Cohan gallery team
Maddie Klett
Belén López
Diana López and Hermán Sifontes
Ramses Mattey
Museum of Modern Art Archives and Library
The New York Public Library
Guillermo Núñez
Michel Otayek
Juan Ignacio Parra Schlageter
Rafael Pastoriza
Carlos Germán Rojas
Rafael Santana
María Inés Sicardi
Sarah Stengel
Vasco Szinetar
Estate of Tecla Tofano
Venezia News
Eduardo Viloria
María Eugenia Zerpa de Córdova

CONTRIBUTORS

AUDRÉE ANID is an artist, curator, and writer. She holds a BA from Wesleyan University in Connecticut and an MA from Teachers College, Columbia University in New York. Audrée has spent over a decade working in the commercial and nonprofit arts sectors of New York City and is currently the director of special projects at James Cohan. While at the gallery, she has curated the group exhibition *Borders* in 2019 and more recently *A Través* in 2022. She has overseen solo exhibitions and global art fair presentations by artists including Gauri Gill, Jordan Nassar, Toshiko Takaezu, Elsa Gramcko, Shinichi Sawada, and Monir Shahroudy Farmanfarmaian. Her projects have been covered by the *New York Times*, the *New Yorker*, *Artforum*, and *New York Magazine*. She is based in Brooklyn, New York.

LUIS FELIPE FARÍAS S. is a lawyer interested in collecting, researching, and promoting the work of Venezuelan artists—particularly women artists and pioneers of modernism whose legacy has been ignored, forgotten, or not sufficiently recognized nationally and internationally. In 2002, he began a comprehensive study of the work of painter and sculptor Elsa Gramcko. Since then he has collaborated with public and private institutions to create exhibitions and publications about the artist, including *Elsa Gramcko, geometría e informalismo* at the Iberoamerican Art Fair in Caracas in 2004, *Contesting Modernity: Informalism in Venezuela, 1955–1975* at the Museum of Fine Arts, Houston, in 2018 and *Elsa Gramcko: The Invisible Plot of Things*, at Sicardi | Ayers | Bacino, Houston, in 2022 and James Cohan, New York in 2023.

LUCÍA HINOJOSA GAXIOLA is an interdisciplinary artist, poet, and editor whose work explores the materiality of language, sound ecology, elements of chance, ritual, and archive. She coedits diSONARE, an experimental editorial project from Mexico City, and is the author of the chapbook *O (Cielo Abierto)* and *The Telaraña Circuit*, an art and poetry book recently published by Tender Buttons. She has exhibited and performed at venues in Mexico City like Museo de Arte Moderno, Vernacular Institute, Centro de la Imagen, and Ex Teresa Arte Actual and in New York City at Microscope Gallery and Essex Flowers, among other places. In 2019 she cofounded RIZOMA, an artist collective offering performance and poetry workshops for imprisoned women in Mexico.

GABRIELA RANGEL is an independent curator, editor, and writer based in New York. Most recently she served as the artistic director of the Museo de Arte Latinoamericano de Buenos Aires. Prior to that she was the visual arts director and chief curator at Americas Society in New York City from 2004 to 2019. She holds an MA in curatorial studies from the Center for Curatorial Studies, Bard College; an MA in media and communications studies from the Universidad Católica Andrés Bello, Caracas; and a BA in film studies from the International School of Film and Television at San Antonio de los Baños, Cuba. She has worked at the Fundación Cinemateca Nacional and the Museo Alejandro Otero in Caracas and at the Museum of Fine Arts, Houston. Gabriela has also curated and cocurated numerous exhibitions on modern and contemporary art that have included work by such artists as Carlos Cruz-Diez, Gordon Matta-Clark, Gego, Arturo Herrera, José Leonilson, and Alejandro Xul Solar. She has written for *Art in America*, *Parkett*, and *ArtNexus*, edited numerous books, and contributed texts to many other art publications.

TECLA TOFANO
THIS BODY OF MINE

Published on the occasion
of the exhibition
Tecla Tofano: This Body of Mine,
curated by Gabriela Rangel
and Audrée Anid at

James Cohan, 291 Grand Street,
New York, NY 10002
November 9–December 16, 2023

Published by
James Cohan, New York
48 Walker Street
New York, NY 10013

EDITORS:
Gabriela Rangel,
Luis Felipe Farías S.
DESIGNER:
Carolina Arnal /
ABV Taller de Diseño
MANAGING EDITOR
AND PRODUCTION:
Todd Bradway
PROJECT MANAGER
(EXHIBITION):
Audrée Anid
TRANSLATIONS:
Lucía Hinojosa Gaxiola
COPYEDITING:
Flatpage
PHOTOGRAPHERS:
Luis Becerra,
Phoebe d'Heurle,
Izzy Leung

Printed and bound by
Faenza Printing SpA, Italy

Printed on Gardamatt 150 g/m²
and Magno Natural 140 g/m²
Typeset in Stempel Schneidler
and Davida

Publication © 2023, James Cohan
Artwork © 2023, Tecla Tofano
All text © 2023, the authors

ISBN: 979-8-218-24093-6
Library of Congress Control
Number: 2023916773

Distributed by
ARTBOOK | D.A.P.
75 Broad Street, Suite 630
New York, NY 10004
Artbook.com

Printed in Italy